a New Land to Live In

Francislee Osseo-Asare

*The Odyssey of an African
and an American
Seeking God's Guidance
on Marriage*

*InterVarsity Press
Downers Grove
Illinois 60515*

InterVarsity Press is the book publishing
division of Inter-Varsity Christian Fellowship,
a student movement active on campus at hundreds
of universities, colleges and schools of
nursing. For information about local and regional
activities, write IVCF, 233 Langdon St.,
Madison, WI 53703.

ISBN 0-87784-722-3
Library of Congress Catalog Card Number: 77-72527

Printed in the United States of America.

To my mother Sylvia & my daughter Abena

Prologue

Part I Naomi

Part II The Stranger's Eyes

Part III Decisions

Special thanks to Ginny Hearn
for her suggestions for
tightening the first draft of the manuscript;
Jeanne Emerson, for her stimulating encouragement;
Beatrice Larbi, for her kindness;
Kwadwo, for being my most
enthusiastic critic.

Prologue

The Bible calls us to be innocent as doves but wise as serpents. When my fiancé and I first discussed marriage, I knew I wanted to be more of a dove than a serpent.

I was in love and all barriers seemed unimportant compared to the immensity of the joy and excitement opened up by our discovery of each other. I preferred trusting in the love passage of 1 Corinthians 13 to reflecting on Jesus' words about counting the cost before building a tower or going into battle.

However, I did recognize that I was also scared. My fiancé was African; I, American. We met in the late 1960s as undergraduates at the University of California, Berkeley. In that environment we realized there were definite implications for two Christians in an interracial, intercultural marriage in the world of the 1970s, a world characterized by growing black/white polarization. Together before God we wrestled to understand what those implications were.

That I was considering marriage to an African committed to returning to his home in Ghana to work, when I had no idea what his home or people were like, frightened me. I had never traveled off the West Coast of the United States. Did *love* and *marriage* even mean the same things in African and American cultures? How did I know that I would be able to make the adjustments required to allow us to live a full life together?

Within a few weeks I knew I had to go to Ghana and spend an extended period of time there. I had to go alone— without my fiancé to continually shield me, to interpret life in his country for me or to initiate all my friendships. I realized I had to go there, live there, work there, meet his family and expose myself to daily life there, before we could make a responsible decision about what to do. Also, my fiancé and I wanted to have time apart from each other to think more fully about what marriage means, and particularly a marriage with the unique demands ours would hold.

When I left California I had just received a B.A. in social work and was preparing to enter graduate school the following year to obtain a master's degree. I needed to go to Ghana, too, to discover if my training was, or could be, relevant to the needs of a newly-independent, developing country.

By working two part-time jobs my last two terms at the University, I was able to save enough money for a round-trip ticket to Ghana. I wrote several letters exploring employment opportunities there. Though I received no favorable replies, I decided to go ahead and make the trip, trusting that God's hand was in our plans and that he would smooth the way. That was the biggest leap of faith I made since my conversion, particularly since I was only able to obtain a fourteen-day tourist visa and had no idea whether I would find a job or be granted a working permit.

In September 1971 I left the San Francisco Bay Area en route to Ghana, via Amsterdam. Upon arriving in Ghana I discovered a letter waiting for me from one of the high schools I had written to inquiring about jobs. I will allow my letters to explain what happened.

The first two sections of this book are taken from my letters and diary during the nine months I spent in a small fishing town along the coast of Ghana. The final section, however, includes excerpts from my fiancé's letters to me and his journal entries as well. In June 1972 he interrupted his graduate studies in metallurgy to meet me in Ghana, and we made a final decision about marrying.

I had always been close to my mother and was deeply hurt to find how greatly my relationship with Kwadwo distressed her. My opening chapter is prefaced by a letter written to me by one of my older sisters when I first telephoned her about my intention to marry Kwadwo. She was herself then living outside the country with a husband who was not born in the United States, and the intensity of her letter eloquently communicates the agony and concern my decision initially caused within my own family.

These letters and journal entries are presented to a wider audience with great trepidation. I am encouraged to offer them largely by the painful memory of a letter I wrote my fiancé after almost nine months in his homeland: "I don't know anyone in Ghana I can talk to about these things." And he replied, "And I on my part don't find anyone here in the States whom I think would understand these things. I trust that out of our experience together others, both in Ghana and the States, will find someone they can talk with should they find themselves in a similar situation."

Francy,

I love you with all my heart and I only want what's best for you. That is why I write this note. It has been about one hour since I talked to you, and what I write is not written to tell you what to do. It's just my thoughts. I hope you look at them honestly, not as prejudiced or permissive, just as coming from someone with little, very little, to judge with, but with your best at heart.

Think of all the times people say, "Look at that white girl with that Negro."

Think of all the white mothers with black babies and how even small children stare.

"Look at that white girl with that Negro."

Think of how hard it will be to accept having a new country, language, background, being away from your family, nice inexpensive stores, the foods you were raised on, the climate you are used to—how hard it is to accept new customs, new everyday life patterns.

"Look at that white girl and that nigger."

Think that he would be the only one you knew—no Shelly, no Linda, no one—and to write would take at least a week each way.

"Look at that white girl with that big nigger."

It is very frightening to have a strange new life where you can't sneak over to the old home to talk it over with mommy.

"Look at that white trash and that big black buck."

Think, I mean really think, about children and know

how very hard it is to raise any child into adulthood and multiply that by two hundred per cent.

"Poor white trash."

Think of all the frightening name-calling and mistrust, the difficulty in choosing friends, in finding places to live. Is this the man to whom you will devote the rest of your life? Whom you will promise to take care of in disease, filth, poverty? Even if these things seem distant, they are very close to everyone.

Do you know how it feels to give up something you really want so badly your heart comes apart? Then to do it again and again. Do you know how to shrink in your mind while he is growing without you? He may shrink, too, you know. Any life has tears, but in marriage there are the most bitter tears of all because any one of these or a million other things can destroy love.

Are you strong enough to support yourself and others through all these things?

My heart knows that it is a thousand times a thousand times harder after it really happens.

Please know mother knows what she is talking about. She knows that it's better to cry for a year than for seventy or even two or five or whatever years. Imagine crying for two years. She knows and she wants you to see through her eyes and head and heart just as I do.

Know that there is no escape from a difficult problem— it's life and must be faced head on. The human being is an extraordinary thing—it can, if it wants, tell itself to believe and do anything, and the body and heart will. It will love, it will suffer, it will forget, it will forget to suffer, and it is only you that can tell it what to do. Do you know you can watch TV and forget this instantly for a moment? You can walk across the street and realize that cool air is heavenly. But can you force yourself again and again to fight down anger, desperation, emotion? Is this a man that you can do this for and is this a man that will help you do it and is this a man that you can say to, "I did it, I did it, I stopped myself from slamming the door!"

How will you feel when you argue and he heads for the bar or takes off in a car at eighty mph? Remember anger can happen to anyone and is a healthy part of a marriage.

I love you.

You will decide for yourself. I can tell you much but it is only this that might help: Now is the time to decide and once decided, let only the truth sway you.

Love, Your sister

Part I
Naomi

. . .Your going away strangely enough reminds me of Naomi. Strange, because in a sense you're going away from me—you're leaving me. Yet not so strange; you're not leaving me. You're going to meet me, my people, my home, the things I've touched in the past, the places you'd previously been exposed to only through your imagination —"Don't ask me to leave you. Your people shall be my people."
(from Kwadwo's first letter to me in Ghana)

Chapter 1
Getting Acquainted

  I had to wait at the Oakland airport three hours to board the plane to Amsterdam. Surrounded by my closest friends, tucked in a deceptive security between my mother and my fiancé, I felt already separated from them all by the trip I had to take alone. A loudspeaker announced my flight number. Relieved by action, the tension of waiting snapped. We exchanged last minute reminders and a rush of hugs: "Remember to return my book to the library." "Write as soon as you can." "Take care of Kwadwo for me." Finally, I turned to Kwadwo. We tried in an embrace, to say everything words no longer could. As I turned away he whispered in my ear, "Christ be with you." As I walked down the ramp to the plane, and many other times over the next ten months, my heart cradled this gift of his to me.

  Now I was Alice, floating down my personal rabbit hole, wondering what would happen next. I looked around and met the inquisitive eyes of a fellow passenger—Alex. As we talked, I learned that he was on his way to Greece. I also learned that he considered himself sufficiently well-informed on African affairs to advise me on my plan to work in Ghana: "I've got a friend who teaches classics at the University of Ghana. His two-year contract was revoked at the end of the first year because of the, ummmm, political situation in Ghana right now. They're trying to force the aliens to leave the country."

I thought of my two-week tourist visa and opened my journal:

First Journal Entry *Sunday, September 5*

The sun is setting now, and I can see blue-gray clouds silhouetted against a rosy orange. There's lightning and flashes of white explode every few minutes. The plane is quieting down and Alex is snoring peacefully. I can't sleep. What happens if I find myself back in Amsterdam after fourteen days? I always want to be in control of a situation. I prefer to trust God only when I can see far enough ahead to be comfortable with the future. Today I've lost that luxury. I've done all I can and must accept the fact that what happens next is out of my hands.

"Thy will be done."

After a brief stopover in Amsterdam I boarded another flight that landed in Nigeria for a few minutes before proceeding to my final destination.

Journal Entry *September 9*

We're at Lagos airport. I'm starting to get excited–in less than an hour we arrive in Accra, the capital of Ghana. The windows fogged up when the plane came down so I can't see anything, except that the mist on them is condensing and little rivers of water are starting to cut thin lines of shifting green in the glass.

First Letter to Kwadwo   *September 9*

Dear Kwadwo,

As I sat down to write you I started crying, partly because I'm tired, but more because I'm overwhelmed by all the good things that have happened.

I arrived in Accra early this morning and was met by a large entourage—Ante Aku at the head. She was shorter and sturdier than I'd imagined, and looks ageless. I felt I ought to do something. So I took some pictures and we all went to Ante Aku's house where she welcomed me with a hearty *"akwaaba"* and the traditional glass of water to a traveler. Then we drank soda and ate cookies (or "minerals" and "biscuits" as you say here). Although I felt conspicuous with everyone coming by to meet and welcome me, I was glad for their friendliness.

This afternoon we went to a school called MODESCO: Modern Secondary and Commercial School. They had not responded to my letter from California but sent a letter to me in care of Ante Aku asking me to come for an interview. They want me to be on their staff! They'll pay my electricity bill, provide free accommodations and allow me at least sixty-five *cedis* [about $65] a month for food and other expenses. I've already decided I like their motto: *Labor Omnia Vincit* (Perseverance Overcomes Everything). God is making crooked paths straight.

There's even more good news. Your sister Afua has been given a complete scholarship to the school for the first term. She'll be able to see if she's interested in learning typing or some other skills. She'll live in the girls' dorm and eat with the other students but be near to help me adjust to life here—and especially to teach me to cook African foods.

Soon we're going to see about having my visa changed.

Love, Adwoa

[In all my letters to Kwadwo I signed my adopted African day name *Adwoa*, meaning I was born on a Monday.]

September 18

Dear Kwadwo,

Ante Aku thinks today will be a bitter memory, but I tried to convince her otherwise. Around 11:00 A.M. we (Ante Aku, Afua and Ante Aku's brother Manu) started for your hometown, Adukrom. The car battery was weak, so we stopped twice to fix it. It wasn't until 12:30 A.M. that we actually began driving to your home. The car slowed to a standstill several times, and before we were halfway Ante Aku was ready to come back to Achimota. Manu kept fixing the car, and we came within a mile of Adukrom before it stopped again. Someone hailed a taxi so that Afua, Ante Aku and I could go on to meet your grandmother while Manu worked on the battery.

Kwadwo, have you ever had the feeling you have been to a place that you could never possibly have seen before? Driving up the mountain, looking at the trees and the mist, I felt strongly that I had seen all this and had stayed here before, perhaps in a dream. Everything looked exactly right. I guess your descriptions were better than I realized. I felt more at home in Adukrom, walking through the red clay in the rain to your parents' old house, than I have felt anywhere else in Ghana. I have been treated well by everyone I have met, and Ante Aku's house and friends are more similar to what I'm used to; yet I felt more myself, more at ease, in Adukrom. I enjoyed talking with your grandmother (even if Afua had to interpret) and meeting people from the town and waving to children laughing as they called out, "*ɔbroni k ɔk ɔ ɔ*" [white person]. It was comfortable.

It is disconcerting, however, to have people make such a big thing out of my being an American—about how ashamed they are of being poor and about how I am sacrificing and on and on. It's all nonsense. People want to treat me differently, like I'm a china teacup and they're unbreakable tin plates. For example, tonight after we returned home Ante Aku and Manu ate *fufu* [pounded plantain and yam], but she cooked me rice instead because "*fufu* is too heavy for *ɔbroni's* stomach." I went over and started eating her dinner instead just to convince her that I like it and that it agrees with me.

When we started to leave Adukrom the car battery finally died completely. We rode another taxi to Ante Aku's hometown a few miles away to wait while Manu went back to Adukrom with a mechanic to recharge the battery. After eating some bread with canned sardines we met hundreds of aunts, uncles and cousins. I struggled through trying to understand their Twi, and people seemed delighted to hear my small conversational repertoire. A lady gave me a boiled yam slice with a thick peppery tomato sauce, and we all sat and talked. A thin old woman sat in a corner chanting, "lone-den, lone-den, lone-den," and clapping bony hands. I finally realized she was singing, "Mɛko Loneden. Mɛko Loneden." ["I'm going to London. I'm going to London."] Was she just enjoying herself, or did she really think that because I'm white I could take her to London?

Love, Adwoa

Journal Entry *September 18*

The people in Adukrom were not so obviously trying—with wigs and cars and refrigerators and rugs and lipstick and fancy dresses— to be "modern."

Except for a few:

The distant, precisely polite, sophisticated young sisters at the bar—here from Accra for a funeral and looking bored.

The young man who claimed to have spent time in Las Vegas studying the casinos, and appeared phony and manipulative with his contrived attentions to me, and in his descriptions of London and Las Vegas.

September 16

Dear Kwadwo,

I was hoping to tell you definitely what has been happening with my visa. I still can't. But Afua and I are staying in a room at MODESCO.

Preparing to move in was a family project:

Yesterday we brought your sisters over in the morning, and they spent all day cleaning the main room, the kitchen and the bathroom. Then your brother Kwaku came after work to scrub the mosquito netting.

While they were working, Ante Aku and I tackled the Ministries again trying to arrange for my residential visa. I'm now moved into the school and working in the office but cannot be legally employed until (that is, if and when) the government approves their request to hire an alien. From what I've seen of the red tape this last week, that could take months. After approval is given (if it is given) I can *apply* for a residential visa. God leads us step by step. . . . When my tourist visa expires I'll simply have to renew it.

Afua is teaching me some more Twi—every day I pick up new words and phrases. I'm also learning how to cook with charcoal and kerosene and live without refrigeration. The weather at this time of year is just like California's, except for the humidity. The things that loomed so frightening in my imagination before, now seem infinitely less formidable. I'm not at all homesick (there is so much to learn and do), but I do miss you.

Love, Adwoa

When I first met Kwadwo's eighteen-year-old sister, Afua, I noted she was thin and limped slightly. Her large, smiling eyes were patient but etched with a pervasive fragility. I learned, during sleepless nights those ten months, of suffering that explained both her wisdom and her too-lean, young-looking frame. I saw pain jab and destroy a rediscovered joy in those eyes as quickly as stones thrown in a quiet pool scatter resting fish. But the fish return, cautiously, and so did her hope.

I never knew how she endured the pain of an inflamed osteomyelitic leg (*osteomyelitis* means "inflammation of the bone") with hopeless operations to remove dead bone, never to cure it, and always being afraid that the doctors would cut it off. I never knew how she survived repeated crises of sickle cell anemia with their stiffening pain that left her crying to me, "Sister Adwoa, I can't, I can't. . . ." She said she couldn't stand it, but somehow she always did.

Emotional crises I knew more about, but not at the level of her everyday experience. Her parents both died while she was a little girl. Their deaths and her illness kept her from continuing her schooling, and sent her to Adukrom to live with the old women and the young children. Her illness toyed with her, sharpening the psychic wounds and scars, the fears of never developing the curves of womanhood or the capacity to bear children, of never knowing financial independence or the trusting dependence of others.

My respect and admiration for Afua grew as I watched her blossom out with a vitality brought by new opportunities, only to be attacked by the blight of disease—and to resist again and again the attack.

September 24

Dear Kwadwo,

. . . Afua will be in the Commercial Division, Form 1, at our school. Since coming to MODESCO she's been eagerly studying Pittman's shorthand, trying to learn all her consonants by the first day of classes. I'm sure she's already written you how the chance to go to school again excites her. She explained to me that you once arranged for her to attend school when you came home to Ghana on a summer vacation, but she became ill during the first term and was

sent home to Adukrom where no one there ever bothered
to send her back to the school. . . .

This morning Afua fell ill. She thinks last night's rain
caused what she calls her "rheumatism" to act up. She'll rest
today and take some of her medicine, indocid. If she isn't
better by tomorrow, I'll take her to the hospital in Tema.
Incidentally, the housemistress here also uses indocid. It
seems her childhood was similar to Afua's—both parents
died and she was sickly. She said that's very African.

I'm glad to be in Ghana to help care for your sister. If you
can't be here, the next best thing is for me to be here for
you.

Love, Adwoa

Journal Entry *September 21*
Still waiting for the visa.

Journal Entry *September 22*
Still waiting for the visa. . . .
*We were up early, and by 7:15 A.M. I was in the headmaster's
office typing. Later I went to the Ministries and was given another
letter—tomorrow I must go again.*

Journal Entry *September 23*
Still waiting for the visa. . . .
*I had my tourist visa extended at the Ministry of Internal Affairs
today while we wait for more news about the residential one. . . .*

Journal Entry *September 23*
*Afua is sitting on the bed singing into my tape recorder. Her
voice is clear and sweet. Listening to her I feel like the unhappy
Keats listening to a nightingale and imagining he is hearing*

Perhaps the self-same song that found a path
Through the sad heart of Ruth, when, sick for home,
She stood in tears amid the alien corn.

As time slips by me I seem to be living in a fog. Things aren't quite real. I'm not at my best. It's too hard to think of things to say to people, and I make too many stupid mistakes. I don't see clearly. It's hard to explain. I need to learn to be fulfilled by taking regular little steps without always wanting to be standing on top of the mountain.

But sometimes, standing "amid the alien corn," I start to get scared and I think—no more closets, no more steaks, no more snow and pine trees, no more freedom from responsibility. . . . And once in a while kenkey [*a heavy, fermented corn dough eaten as the starch with stew or fried fish*] *seems to choke me, or the thought of fishheads or snails or more tomato sauce for the rest of my life frightens me.*

. . . I miss Kwadwo. I miss my family and friends. Last night I discovered I had a tape recording of my four-year-old sister Michelle singing "Jingle Bells." It filled me with a painful warmth and a desire to be with certain people again. I guess this is homesickness.

School opens tomorrow.

Chapter 2
Schoolteacher

Dear Kwadwo,

School reopened yesterday, and everything turned to noise and activity as the boarding students began arriving. A steady stream of trucks and trunks flowed around the dormitories all day, and the air was filled with shouts of recognition as reunions took place. I have now been officially introduced to everyone as the new assistant housemistress. I smile to think that only three months ago I was a student myself. I do wonder, though, why everyone always warns me about insubordination and encourages me to put the "fear of God" into the students as if it were penicillin.

Tonight there was a variety show. There were lots of in-jokes I didn't understand, but everyone seemed to have a good time. There wasn't much real singing, mostly catcalls and laughter, talking and clapping. I seemed quite an object of interest and the students unexpectedly requested a song from me. Red-cheeked as the Campbell Soup Kid, I picked a Peter, Paul and Mary folk song I hoped they wouldn't know the tune to and was relieved when the housemaster thanked me after the first stanza. It was natural to think about you tonight, too, and wonder what you were like when you entered secondary school and later when you were a prefect. I think that some of the older boys here consider themselves prefects from the arrogant way they act.

Another change occurred today too. Afua moved her bed to an upstairs dormitory. Due to her shyness and fear of being bullied by the senior students, she had wanted to continue to sleep in my room and be a day student. We have worked everything out now, though, and she seems content. While it's strange to be by myself again after two and a half weeks, I like the return of that familiar feeling of privacy.

Incidentally, whether the school will finally be authorized to employ me is still not decided. While I wait, I've extended my tourist visa fourteen more days. The headmaster and proprietor of the school have already gone to the Ministry of Education twice to try and have the matter settled, and one of Ante Aku's inexhaustible supply of friends is trying to help us too.

We walk by faith not by sight. I am comforted knowing I can look back and see that God has led us step by step—no leaps and bounds but many inches adding up to literally thousands of miles.

Please keep writing. Your letters mean more than I can tell you.

Love, Adwoa

Journal Entry *September 26*

It looks like freshmen initiations are unfortunately not reserved to the United States. The senior girls are forcing the "homos"–the new students—to march around the compound. Through my open window I can see they have made the girls unplait their hair and leave it uncombed, put white powder on their faces, and sing and clap as they go. Both the housemistress and the housemaster are off-campus now, so the house prefects have power to do as they wish.

I'm too unfamiliar with the system here to know how to respond, and this may very well be a perfectly acceptable tradition. Still, it reminds me too much of my own first week of junior high school: Some eighth-grade bullies pushed my textbooks into a garbage can in the girls' bathroom and forced me to try to get them out, laughing at me because I was too short to reach to the bottom of the can. I had an eighth-grade sister to rescue me, but how can I protect these girls?

September 24

Dear Kwadwo,

... We eat simple meals here—bread and tea or rice-water or *koko* [porridge] in the morning, and lots of fish (since we're right next to the sea we can buy six fish for ten cents— I mean, *pesewas*) and rice and yams. I can't tell fried African yams from fried potatoes. This afternoon we had *nkatenkwan* (or however you spell peanut soup) and rice, and tonight *nkontomire* stew (is *nkontomire* spinach?) with fried plantains and yams. Delicious! Aren't you jealous?

I find living without closets or refrigerators or hot water to be a relatively small matter. After visiting Adukrom I'm thankful for running water and electricity. However, I've yet to decide who's winning—me or the mosquitoes. I think we're about even.

Things aren't rushed here (it's been an adjustment getting used to the slow, relaxed pace of life), but days are full, from early until late. I seem to get tired easily too. Could it be the humidity? ...

Love, Adwoa

September 26

Dear Kwadwo,

The students had their first morning chapel service today. Everyone seemed to be dressed in white except a few of the boys who were wearing traditional cloths draped around themselves. The beautiful a cappella singing was fresh and much more energetic than we North Americans usually produce. One of the seniors preached, but my attention quickly wandered back to you, imagining you preaching while you were at Achimota Secondary School.

Though chapel was compulsory not all the students were there—some of the girls were hiding out in their dorms. Already over fifty girls have arrived, and it will be quite a job to supervise them. I'm glad I'm just the assistant. The new housemistress plans to retire from teaching and spend time just being with the girls. She speaks Ga along with most of the students, as well as Ewe. Probably in her fifties, she seems quite competent, and I'm sure I'll learn much from her.

In fact today before chapel she showed me how Ghanaian women dress. First she put on her skirt—carefully wrapping the long piece of cotton cloth around her before tying a thin string over it at her waist. Then she put on a simple overblouse and draped a folded cloth over one shoulder. After I'm paid I'll buy some material from Makola market in Accra. Afua and I can use the old hand-operated Singer machine that belonged to your mother to sew a traditional Ghanaian outfit.

Classes start next week. The more I'm with the students, the more relaxed I feel and the better able to move beyond my anxiety about what kind of a teacher I'll be. I hope to catch on quickly to the teaching methods and the material I'm to cover. Besides teaching English language, typing and Bible Knowledge classes, I'll be working part-time in the office as an administrative assistant to the headmaster, particularly doing typing, receptionist work and establishing a filing system in the office. There seems to be only one other full-time staff person here with a bachelor's degree. The other teachers seem to have completed at most their O- or A-level exams.

Oh yes, I'm still waiting for confirmation from the Ministry of Education about my job here.

Love, Adwoa

October 1

Dear Kwadwo,

My first day of teaching was traumatic. It would have been funny if I hadn't lost my sense of humor somewhere between here and Berkeley. We don't have any stationery or books yet, and there were to be no classes: "Just go in for a minute and introduce yourselves to your Form (homeroom) and welcome them," the headmaster told us.

My first class was English, Form 2B—many of the students in the class entered the school in Form 1 last year when MODESCO opened. They were excited about the "white lady from America" and everyone was waiting to see which classes I would have. I paused outside the door to take a deep breath and regret again that my cheeks turn so red on all important occasions. (In one of their first essays, several of the students described me as having "blue eyes and red skin.")

I walked smiling into the classroom. Immediately about thirty-five boys and girls cheerfully bounced up from their seats, and I heard a chorus of, "Good morning, mistress." I went in, said a few words and had the distinct impression that the students didn't understand me. I imagine English as a second language is difficult enough without also having to contend with my American accent. When I took a piece of chalk and wrote my name on the board I was even more unnerved to hear a wave of giggling rise behind me. [At the time I couldn't appreciate how amusing, and slightly inappropriate, it seemed to them to see a schoolmistress write with her left hand. Traditionally the right hand is for eating, writing, extending gifts and so on, while the left hand is used for personal hygiene. I picked up on this custom when Afua later refused to let me cook left-handed.]

As quickly as I thought decent I dismissed the class and hurried out of the room. After talking outside with one of the other teachers, I was advised to stay with the students and have a discussion. So I turned around and walked back into the classroom, feeling silly. The students may have been confused, but they good-naturedly jumped to attention again, and I attempted to lead a discussion. The conversation lagged, and with relief I heard one of the seniors walk by ringing a bell to signal the end of class. I felt discouraged until a fellow teacher told me about his own frustrations the first term he taught. I decided I just needed to relax.

Tuesday was much better. I told the class about my home in California. Saturday night one of the girls had sung "Oh My Darling, Clementine" at the variety show, so I described how this song and "Oh, Susannah" were from the gold rush days in California and what the gold rush was like. Then they asked me earnestly about President Kennedy's death and black-white problems in the United States. Thursday (still no teaching) their master hadn't come during my free period, so I spent it with them and we had a spelling bee. They begged me to stay with their class and not go to my next period.

In my other classes I asked students about their names and had them tell me about where they were from and what their favorite foods were. They were surprised to learn that I like Ghanaian cooking and pleased that I ate in the dining hall with them one day. The oldest students I teach are in Form 3, and the class is Bible Knowledge. We had a lively discussion when I asked them if it is important to spend so much time studying the Bible. I talked about the Pharisees who studied the Law for years yet how Jesus condemned them for their ignorance. They had never thought about it. Afua is in one of my typing classes too. I'm sure now that I'll enjoy teaching.

Love, Adwoa

October 12

Dear Kwadwo,

MODESCO is just entering its second year of existence and we still teach in "temporary" indoor/outdoor classrooms made of wood and covered with corrugated tin roofs. The rooms let in fresh air, but unfortunately, along with that a little rain and a lot of noise from the other classrooms. There are never quite enough desks or benches either, and each morning after the benches are moved into the large hall for chapel there is a flurry of tugging as everyone rushes to regain his or her seat and return it to his classroom. My classes seem to increase in size every day—they've almost reached the forty mark now—and several students have to share benches, which always leads to extra giggling and pushing in class.

The girls are supposed to wear pale blue dresses to school and the boys white or pastel shirts with blue slacks. The school administration keeps making announcements about "proper attire," but a large minority of students who wear clothes other than the required uniforms aren't penalized. (However, the assistant headmaster frequently threatens the boys for wearing flashy rings and necklaces.) The reason for the lack of uniforms is undoubtedly the same as for the lack of textbooks, even basic texts like English books or typing manuals: students' parents simply can't afford another twenty *cedis* [about $20] on top of the tuition and fees and, for some, the boarding fees too.

The permanent buildings that make up MODESCO are two large cement houses—one contains the headmaster's office, the staff common room and the boys' dormitories. The second building holds the girls' dormitories and the living quarters for both the housemistress and myself. I enjoy standing on the covered patio outside my room to look at the morning-glories climbing the fence or the bougainvillea dancing up the trellis along one end of the patio. In the evenings, especially, there are numerous sheep that play or rest in the grass in front of the porch, surrounded by the shadows of the house and mango trees.

About midway between the two buildings there is a single faucet where the boarding students fill their buckets twice a day for bathing. The bathing and latrine facilities for the students are all separate from the dormitories. Fortunately, the housemistress and I have our own shower and toilet facilities to share, and separate kitchens with running water. There's no water heater but the weather is warm enough that cool showers in the morning are refreshing.

My living-bed-dining room is ten blue linoleum tiles wide by eighteen tiles long. It's furnished with my cot, two chairs and Afua's trunk. Afua and I both have small wooden tables that double as desks in it too. I keep my clothes in a box under the bed, right next to the suitcase I brought with me. Finally, we have a small wooden cabinet where we keep some of our food—tea, Bournvita, marmalade, margarine and so on. There's a small, friendly lizard—you call them "housemothers" don't you?—that has moved into the upper corner of one of our blue cement walls and keeps me company.

Love, Adwoa

October 14

Dear Kwadwo,

I'm sitting in one of the temporary classrooms trying to prepare lessons. It's peaceful and the palm trees are waving at me. Several chickens are wandering in the grass, and two boys are playing table tennis just outside the door. Some carpenters are sawing in the distance. The wooden desk under this aerogram was new a month ago, but now it is covered with the doodling of many students—"my name is Mr. Nobody," "Yesterday, yesterday, yesterday" (words from a popular song), "We shall overcome," "Busia" (the Prime Minister), Agnes Acquaye (one of my students), "Yesterday, today, forever, Jesus is the same" (undoubtedly a message from one of the Scripture Union members and also the title to a chorus in the Scripture Union songbook), "The Best University in Africa," "$72 \times 5 = 360$" and so on.

I'm worried about the behavior of some of the senior students. I've had a feeling since the first week of school that some of the prefects were irresponsible. I guess that when the school began last year students were accepted for Forms 1-5 rather than beginning with just first year students only and growing each year. Probably the administration felt it could not financially afford to wait several years until all five forms were filled. The result has been that a number of students who were expelled from one or more other secondary schools have been admitted into the senior grades here. The decision to admit them has had serious consequences.

For example, yesterday one of the prefects took a heavy belt and whipped all the students in Forms 1 to 3 during dinner. One of the younger girls ran and hid in my room. The seniors insist that the younger students refuse to respect them and are completely undisciplined. And, of course, the juniors accuse the seniors of cruelty. My sympathies are with the junior students. The prefects certainly on the whole are not setting a good example for the other students in self-discipline. Also, I understand the male prefects have established a "Firing Squad" off in some obscure corner of the school where they beat students who have fallen into their disfavor.

I strongly oppose the violent tactics of these "leaders"

and wish it were possible to discipline the senior prefects. We did have a staff meeting discussing the bullying going on, but no action was decided upon. Again, I think the administrators cannot afford to expel any paying students. Incidentally, through all these incidents Afua has been left untouched. They're afraid she'll tell me if they hurt her. In fact they've nicknamed her "Busia's daughter," after the Prime Minister, meaning she has a special relationship with someone who can protect her. . . .

Love, Adwoa

October 15

Dear Kwadwo,

Today is another first.

For the first time I have on Ghanaian dress. Afua took this dress out of her trunk to show me, along with the few gold necklaces of your mother that she and Ama were able to salvage after her death.

Afua wrapped the cloth around her just like the housemistress had, then slipped into the sleeveless blouse. She said you call the outfit *kabba ne ntama* and offered to let me try it on. It's so comfortable and has such pretty colors— yellow stripes with touches of green and bands of deep violet and black. Afua made it herself and was happy it fit me even though I'm bigger than she is. She suggested I wear it. Though I had been on my way outside I hesitated for several minutes, steeling myself to endure the stares of the students and being nervous about my lack of grace in walking in it.

It wasn't too painful. Everyone complimented me (naturally) and told me how Ghanaian I looked and how it was perfect for me. Later Afua and I went to buy some kerosene. The lady who always sells to us was so happy to see me in *kabba ne ntama* that she "dashed" us (treated us to) four oranges and a piece of chewing gum. Kwadwo, *me pɛ Ghana papaapa* [I like Ghana very much]. . . .

Love, Adwoa

October 18

Dear Kwadwo,

Let me tell you about the men behind the school. The manager, the bursar and the assistant headmaster were all friends in various positions who lost their jobs after the coup when Nkrumah was ousted. Last year the manager, who owns the land and buildings here, decided to start his own school. He rounded up his friends and together they entered this venture.

The assistant headmaster is especially hard-working. He seems to be the cement holding the school together, though at the expense of his health—he stays up all night sometimes and makes himself sick overworking. He's a thin, nervous man, with sunken cheeks. Every day he can be found in his office, sitting on one of the three padded chairs crowded around the long table, immersed in the clutter of paper, folders, books and miscellany. He speaks sharply to the students and often threatens them, yells or fires questions at them, but they know he's harmless. Newcomers get flustered when he waves them out of the room with one hand without even looking at them, but soon they learn that he's gentle and good-natured.

The manager is a big man with an impassive face. He always acts grave and distant around me. I imagine the school is an awful financial burden on him. The last couple of days about ten of his thirty sheep died, too, and he is worried about the rest. I wouldn't want to be as pressured as he is.

The bursar's office isn't even in the same part of the building, so I see him least. All I know is that he's always smiling or laughing and seems to work well with the other men.

The acting headmaster is much younger than any of the other men, in his mid-to-late twenties, and is also the least committed to the school. MODESCO is just a wayside stop for him. While he's pleasant to me, he isn't overly interested in what goes on here. I imagine he'll leave as soon as something better turns up.

Several of the teachers here are part-time teachers from other schools in the area. One of them, the head of our English department, irritates me incredibly. He seems to think he's superior to everyone he meets, and I always feel like he's showing off his beautiful English by making empty, windy speeches or condescending terribly to sit at the same table with another person. Despite his personality, the man is unquestionably intelligent and probably an excellent teacher.

One of the other teachers also makes me uncomfortable. A part-time teacher from the Academy of Sciences, he acts very interested in me—wanting to take me to the movies and show me around. He's too friendly and I've been discouraging him. He told me how a friend of his "went all the way to Europe to get him a white wife." When he saw your picture in my room (he knows I'm engaged), he smiled conspiratorially and said, "So you like African men, eh?" We're on totally different wavelengths. . . .

Love, Adwoa

October 20

Dear Kwadwo,

Today I visited Tema with Ante Aku and one of your cousins. We went first to the large government-supported Tema Secondary School where Ante Aku's daughter is a student. It's quite a switch from humble little MODESCO! Next we drove by Valco and around the industrial area to the fishing harbor and finally to the popular Meridian Hotel. Upstairs in the air-conditioned bar where Odami and I went for a few minutes, there were more white faces than I've seen together since I arrived in Ghana. Everyone was sipping his or her afternoon cocktail. Perhaps Odami liked it, but I didn't want to stay. I was angry that the rich white tourists and businessmen were in there at all. (Actually, I was angry the rich blacks were there too.) I sound strange. . . . It's funny, I haven't met but two Europeans or Americans since I arrived. I guess we hang out in different hotels.

There is something I've missed in Ghana. For the first time in my life I've been lonely. There are many people around, but no one to share deeply with. I recognize the loneliness and am trying to use initiative to make friends rather than choosing to get depressed. I find myself isolated from many of your old friends. I did see Franklin Dove twice, weeks ago, but he's the only friend of several you told me about that I've even met. I haven't been very mobile so far, and friendships will have to come from new directions. Today I stayed at school because Grace (a good friend of your fellow Ghanaian, Kwamena, at Berkeley) promised she would come see me today, but it's 4:00 P.M. and she isn't here yet. However, I am getting to know various people at the school—the housemaster and housemistress and some of the teachers.

Being here only a few weeks I can already recognize that it will be a stiff challenge to maintain our ideals of non-materialism when we return to Ghana, just as it will be important and difficult to learn humility. As soon as the magic Ph.D. is tacked onto your name or I have an MSW, people will want to treat us even more differently.

Perhaps because I haven't been running with the university crowd I haven't yet found any of the overt hostility I was anticipating. Rather, it's been the other extreme—people staring in admiration or sitting up straighter or pointing me out to others. Parents or other visitors who come to MODESCO always hear of the "B.A. from America coming to help the school." At first I didn't like to be singled out and conspicuous, but if I'm completely honest I have to admit that part of me does like it. Regardless of my arguments, it makes me feel important even though I know— better than anyone else—the shallow meaning of the degree "with honors." Pray for me. I need to keep close watch on my ego.

Love, Adwoa

Chapter 3
Religion and Christianity

While an undergraduate at the University of California I had discovered a group of students committed to thinking through and living out the implications of their Christian faith. As this fellowship was important in the development of my understanding of the gospel, I looked forward to involvement with a similar group at the secondary school level in Ghana. From Kwadwo I knew the organization I wanted to locate was called the Scripture Union or simply SU.

After I was hired, I sought out MODESCO's energetic, enthusiastic SU patron (a young faculty member) who was delighted to meet me and acted disconcertingly as if I'd been expected. At the students' first SU meeting I was both observer and participant. I admired the easy leadership of my faculty colleague, Brother Adjei, and his effortless rapport with the students.

After the meeting closed Brother Adjei confided to me

that though he'd taught at MODESCO the year before, he would soon be leaving and had been praying earnestly that God would bring a qualified replacement to the school. He'd been wondering who would come, and now here I was. Within a week he resigned to attend one of the universities in Ghana, assured that God was leading me and the SU group. I was less confident. I'd been expecting Brother Adjei to meet my needs, and before I even had the opportunity to express them I was the "patron" of the SU.

In the coming weeks the newly-adopted role of SU advisor in a foreign culture (and without any formal preparation) precipitated a necessary crisis in my own spiritual life. Innumerable threads began twisting themselves into a rope that wound itself around me like a noose.

Choking me was the religion of prohibition. The students had, in many ways, been exposed to a narrow, distorted Christianity. I recognized it as similar to the approach so prevalent in sections of the evangelical community in my own country. It appeared to me that the role in this religion assigned to me was that of "the white missionary lady."

I was neither to drink, to dance nor to wear jeans. I was to smile eternally and thrive on fire and brimstone tracts stressing God's judgment, mediocre evangelistic music imported from America and various religious pieties. I was to require the same behavior from the students, especially the SU members. I was not to encourage students to think about why and what they believed.

Confused, timid and conforming, I strenuously attempted to convince myself that I really thought all dancing was wrong, or at least an important issue. In misguided efforts to keep from being a stumbling block I refused to drink even a glass of beer. Wanting to assimilate, I unconsciously tried to become who I thought everyone else wanted me to be. But a hollowness, an intense frustration and sense of hypocrisy began to surface over the weeks. It took many months for God to free me from my partially self-imposed, partially externally-imposed, noose.

October 9

Dear Kwadwo,

... Mr. Adjei, the former SU patron, has now officially resigned from the school. He was here long enough to introduce me to the SU members but not long enough to get me used to the idea of being the head of the group.

I feel inadequate and my two initial contacts with the SU have been disappointing. Last Sunday I led our first Bible study. It was on Nehemiah. While a large number of students showed up, almost no one besides me did any talking. And I had planned on an *inductive* study! I still don't know what the problem is/was, and all my questions only lead me to my knees.

The second contact was yesterday. One of the SU members invited me to talk about Christian life in the United States at the club meeting that afternoon. I agreed, thinking I'd have time during my free periods to prepare. Well, I got stuck in a board of directors meeting (I'm secretary and had to take minutes) that ended just in time for me to walk into an overflowing room of regular SU members and other curious students. I prayed a quick prayer with the group, asking God to lead us, and then began talking about anything that came to mind. As I jumped lamely from one topic to another I watched the blank faces of the students. Couldn't they understand my English? Were they being polite? Did they expect me to tell them the United States was a utopia? What was wrong? There were no miracles whatsoever. I felt panicky because I seemed to have trusted God about everything but nothing was happening. Finally I asked the students to sing. They stood up and I said a few words about what the words to the songs meant. Then the meeting closed. I felt ashamed that I'd failed God again.

Franklin Dove, your classmate, dropped by that very afternoon and comforted me greatly, both with his presence and a book he brought me. We talked and shared for hours. Maybe God heard my prayer after all?

Please pray with me for an upsurge of the Holy Spirit among the Christians here that will fill the school with agape. To begin to pray like that, when as far as you can see all is emptiness, is faith. . . .

Love, Adwoa

October 19

Dear Kwadwo,

. . . Last Saturday I was invited to be one of three speakers at an SU leadership conference in a secondary school in Accra. My topic? Christ's leaders. How ironic! It forced me to think through just what a leader is in God's eyes. It was helpful to remind myself that throughout history he has often chosen people to do certain tasks for which they feel ill-prepared. I'm not the first one, anyhow!

However, I realize now how much time I wasted at conferences and retreats back home. I never knew that some day I'd be in this position. A good strong wind has blown away my crutches and forced me down before the One who sent the wind. Rev. Palmer at First Pres back home once talked about how a crisis situation (like Jesus always poses) is good because it forces you to see what is most important by clearing away the trivia. That's what's happening to me. Things seem to be getting clearer.

Last week, for example, I led the students in morning worship every day. With no books to quote (except the Bible!) and not even a concordance, I'm forced to pray and take my discipleship more and more seriously. Thank God for that. Also, there is a positive side to those several discouraging sessions I've had with the SU. Rather than jump out all enthusiastic about my amazing abilities, I'm having to try to understand what it means to wait on God. Remember:

> *They that wait upon the Lord shall renew their strength;*
> *they shall mount up with wings as eagles;*
> *they shall run, and not be weary;*
> *they shall walk, and not faint.*

(Isaiah 40:31, KJV)

Love, Adwoa

October 20

Dear Kwadwo,

Our housemaster has seen me talking with the SU students and thus discerned that I'm "interested in spiritual things." He is too. A slender, excitable young man with intense eyes, he's a dedicated spiritualist who sees himself as gifted with miraculous powers from God. He dreams only of getting a VW bus, gathering together some people he knows and traveling around the country doing "evangelistic" work. He apparently thinks I'm God's instrument to help him obtain the money he needs and wants me to get him in touch with some spiritualists in California so they can back him. His large eyes positively glow in an eerie way when he shares his ambitions. I'm confused about just how his spiritualism and Christianity come together though. While he uses familiar words, like "Lord," "Jesus Christ as Savior" and others, he is infatuated with the ability he claims he has to knock people down on the ground by praying. I told him of my skepticism but agreed to attend a meeting with him at a spiritual church near here.

I'm convinced the housemaster is at least partially involved with another problem at the school. Certain students and anonymous masters (I suspect it's the housemaster) have set themselves up as "prophets and prophetesses" whose duty it is to point out the wizards, witches and satans among us. One of the students involved is also an outspoken, if immature, member of the SU, who even accompanied me to that SU leadership conference last week. Unfortunately, the prophet(s) and prophetess(es) are sowing hostility and dissension throughout the school, especially among the more naive students.

I gather, though, that I've not yet been accused of being a witch. Rather, the students go to the other extreme. With all my blatant inadequacy and even though I fail in front of them, the students believe God has brought me here to lead them. Last week an evangelist made contact with the school because he felt God was calling him here. The first thing he was told was that God has brought a white lady from America to be a teacher here and that she is a "born again believer" who has started a revival in the school. The revival part is not quite accurate, in my opinion, and I distinctly disliked the intimation that somehow, because I'm white or American, I'm more qualified to be a Christian.

Anyhow, back to problems in the school, the senior house prefect and his assistant have been suspended for two weeks and removed from their offices for the recent beating and bullying of the junior students. The assistant is a Christian and SU member. He told me privately that he was in turmoil about what was going on but felt helpless to stop it without the support of the other seniors. Though *something* has been done, I don't think the basic problem—the attitudes of many of the seniors—has been resolved yet.

Love, Adwoa

October 5

Dear Kwadwo,

I asked my Form 3 students in Bible Knowledge (BK) to write an essay in class on "What Is Religion?" I'm just beginning to correct the papers, but they already show that either they don't understand the concept of religion, or they're not able to express their thoughts about it clearly

in English. Many said things like, "Religion is Bible reading" or "In the olden days people didn't have religion"
or "Religion is the study of the Bible and our Lord Jesus
Christ as Savior." Perhaps they were just trying to tell me
what they thought I wanted to hear. If so, they were wrong.

Yesterday when I went to class I told them I just wanted
us to talk about religion because I don't think most of them
really know what it is. After stating that religion is not
simply the same thing as Christianity, I went on to explain
that all people everywhere must answer certain questions—
about life, death, suffering, meaning, evil, goodness and so
on. These are the things that are important to us. Besides
referring to other major world religions, I broadened my
definition to include such things as humanism and personal
idolatries. What seemed to interest them was the idea that
each one of them could be expressing a personal religion
whether he realized it or not. Many students began our discussion with the assumption that pleasure is the highest
good, so things were lively. . . .

Love, Adwoa

P.S. My visa expired again today but I continue to tackle the
red tape surrounding the residence permits.

October 15

Dear Kwadwo,

I was excited to go to my BK class today. We're supposed
to study various world religions briefly this term before we
begin looking at one of the Synoptic Gospels next term. As I
wrote you, last week when I explained the kinds of religious
questions man faces they seemed interested. Today when I
continued, repeating that Christianity was one answer, and
Buddhism and fetishism and Confucianism and Islam and
humanism other answers, I thought everyone was going to
fall down dead. Some of the students were hopelessly confused. Many were upset and kept saying things like, "We

want to use the Bible" or "This is BK class." They really didn't want to listen to what I was talking about. I tried to share a poem I wrote when I was their age expressing my belief that somewhere there was something higher than myself and that there was meaning, even though I didn't know what it was then. I only succeeded in throwing the students deeper into a panic. I finally read to them from this term's syllabus to convince them I was following it, and they calmed down some. But at first you would have thought I was the antichrist.

I was upset, too. But the more I think about it the less upset I am. Many of these students are at best nominal Christians who have never thought much about their faith, particularly one girl and boy who clamored the loudest.

The girl, the daughter of a Ghanaian mother and an English father (who are separated), dreams only of going to Hollywood to become a movie star. She heard I was having a prayer meeting with some of the girls last night, so she nonchalantly bounced into my room with a long stick of incense burning in her hair, then left and returned later to hear more about the glories of the United States. I'm sure I disappointed her.

The boy's name is Michael. Like the girl, he's personable and entertaining. He's also tall, good-looking, popular, a good dancer, the life of the party and much admired for his ability to sing soul music.

Though both students put on serious and indignant faces in class today, they were just playing games. I felt sad. I thought, "Who am I to judge the authenticity of their walk with God?" I felt like a hypocrite and was afraid it was my pride that allowed them to upset me.

Then I realized that I was attacking their religion—the westernized institutional church complete with morning chapel. I was challenging, most of all, their adopted tradi-tion. I found I didn't want to upset them. I was ready to run to a nice noncontroversial book and stay hidden in it. However, if religion, in the churchianity sense of the word, cannot give life, if it is on a par with all the manmade religions of the world, then I shouldn't worry about upsetting the students. If I'm destroying a genuine faith they have, it's an entirely different matter. I must be careful. I remember James's words: "Let not many of you become teachers, my brethren, for you know that we who teach shall be judged with greater strictness" (Jas. 3:1). I must not criticize without offering the students something better.

How ironic, though, that students are forced to take BK in the hopes that they'll become "better Christians" when they probably don't have any idea that it's anything more than a matter of memorizing facts for an examination! As Isaiah said,

This people honors me with their lips,
but their heart is far from me;
in vain do they worship me,
teaching as doctrines the precepts of men.
   (Mt. 15:8-9)

It's so hard to swim upstream though. After I realized I disliked sitting up on a platform before the students every morning during chapel (they line the teachers up facing the students, presumably to add an air of solemnity and authority), I decided just to sit with the students on the benches. The other teachers and students still make comments about why don't I like to take my proper seat. I'm sure they think I'm overidentifying with the students. In the first place, though I haven't told anyone, I find the whole morning worship pretty meaningless—though I do enjoy the singing. I also don't think some should be up above the others simply because they are teachers, especially if we're holding morning "worship." Now I've begun to wish I'd never gone against this tradition. Maybe next time I'll just quietly and humbly step up to the platform?

I also find that the tracts the SU students like to hand out don't move me, though they undoubtedly touch other people's lives. I came to God not simply out of fear for my soul because I might die and go to hell but because I encountered God's love. I can't use words that aren't mine. The evangelist who visited us last week received a strong response to a message I never could have preached, and a message that left me unmoved. When I ask what "Living Water" or "Bread of Life" God will let me give, I feel weak and impotent. What can I do?

Love, Adwoa

November 3

Dear Kwadwo,

Many of the students take their cue from the masters here who give lip service to the Christian faith. They accept Christ's teachings as a vague moral code or an abstract faith but have no concept of what a daily relationship with the Risen Lord might mean. Everyone is looking for the good life (money, good times and so on) and thinks he or she is too sophisticated for Christianity. They certainly don't want a faith that places demands on their lifestyles—the SU students are frequently laughed at and looked down on as "holy holys." I've sometimes overheard the comment, "As if we don't get enough religion here already." I sympathize with that last remark. The problem is that Christ is not the same as much of what's dished up here as Christianity.

I'm somewhat frustrated with the text that was finally assigned for our BK class too. It's a simple book by a professor from the Department for the Study of Religions at the University of Ghana, Legon. His comparative approach allows the students to conclude that religion is basically a moral code and that all religions come up with the same tenets, more or less—love one another, do good, don't do evil and so on. They are complacent about the miracles Jesus could do that some other religious leaders couldn't. Most aren't too concerned one way or another about the possibility of Jesus being unique. Their lives aren't touched.

The students spend hours preparing for confirmation, a huge social event in their lives. But it's a spiritually meaningless acquisition. The day before his confirmation, Michael was caught sneaking out of the dining hall with about five loaves of bread under his shirt. He treated the whole matter as a joke, yet taking extra bread for himself literally means some of the students would have gone hungry.

Of course I confess that there is a certain irrepressible and irreverent humor the students possess, which is refreshing. I'm trying to let them know where I stand while responding to such statements in class as, "Excuse me, mistress, but if Mary and Joseph were only engaged, well then, how did Jesus . . . er, I don't understand where he came from." This student surely knew the doctrine of the Virgin Birth already. He was just entertaining his classmates by the implicit sexual undertones of his question and waiting to see how I'd answer. (Incidentally, I decided to keep a straight face and respond, "Why yes, that's a very good question. I'm glad you asked. It's bothered theologians and lay people for many years." I then went on to discuss the Virgin Birth.) The same student then proceeded to ask me if I thought Mary Magdalene was Jesus' girl friend. (I wonder if he'd been listening to *Jesus Christ, Superstar?*) . . .

Love, Adwoa

During my stay in Ghana I gradually discovered a new joy in solitude, a new awareness of the generous beauty of nature. She gave of herself freely, spoke words I could understand, accepted me and demanded nothing.

Mornings I meditated in a shack tucked illegally in a corner of the campus where barefoot children came late in the day to learn the alphabet and sing. In the evenings, while the students were dining or sleeping, I developed the habit of climbing the winding lighthouse-style steps to the roof of the girls' dormitory. The girls were strangely afraid of the narrow stairs and only once followed me. The roof became my sanctuary, with its clear view of meadows, palm trees and the sea. Later I slept there on hot nights (much to the consternation of several girls who felt I was exposing myself to the witches flying through the night air).

In solitude, with a growing need for communication, my prayers took on a new quality. I poured out my heart to God and listened earnestly for his voice.

October 12

Dear Kwadwo,
 I just watched sunset: God's candle
 Golden blue and orange and soft pink wax melting,
 Changing colors in flickering light.
 The flame slipped down
 And went out, leaving twilight—
 Its silent benediction.
The beauty left me thinking of you. Every part of the day (and night) here is beautiful. I go out alone in the morning to pray before sunrise when there is a stillness and freshness over everything that reminds me God is a God of peace and harmony. When the light breaks baptizing the world for the day's work there is brightness and warmth, and the flowers laugh gaily. In the afternoon the sea breezes blow the tall grass. It bows down with a perfect rhythm and sweet smell. I've written you of the evening before. Have I ever spoken of the stars? They're closer here, and brighter, with no streetlights to dim them. Or the sea? I can see its serene blue and turquoise tapestry from the roof where I sit. . . .

Love, Adwoa

Journal Entry *October 22*

I've come again this morning to the primary school to pray and read my Bible. This little school—the rusty corrugated tin and weathered plywood with holes in it, the red dirt floor, the low uneven benches—is becoming a part of me.

I just read 1 Kings—about Elijah and the still, small voice he heard in the cave. God wasn't in the wind or the earthquake or the fire. Too often I want wind or a mighty blaze, and so I turn away from that quiet voice to look for a show. God, help me to hear you speak.

A boy in Form 3 was here praying this morning when I came. After sharing a brief prayer, he left . . . then came back. He really wants to talk to me about how he can get to America, not to God.

Journal Entry *November 8*

My life seems to be calling out to me tonight. I try to sleep but keep waking to wipe the sweat from my face and hopelessly push damp hair from my neck. The wetness stays. The night is hot and I turn over and over, trying to find some coolness on the limp and dingy yellowed sheet. Now on my back I wait for the buzz of mosquitoes to attack my ears and force me to cover myself with sticky cloth. Then I roll over and try to hide my head under the pillow, but more warmth seems to suffocate me and my nose clogs so I can't breathe.

Tonight God seems to be so near and Satan is even closer. It frightens me but I can't say how. So many thoughts come and move away from this pen. . . .

God is so much more, and I push him away by dishonesty. I don't bring the real questions that tear at me, and so I don't find him. Did mosquitoes bite Jesus? Did he find some nights too hot to sleep? Did he sweat and wipe the dirt from himself? Did he know about . . . how life is? I have such a rigid unreal knowledge of him. What would he do in a world like MODESCO? We all glibly speak about salvation, and then in our rooms and in our souls we find we're so different from the Jesus we know too little of. . . .

November 12

Dear Kwadwo,

... This week I picked up the book I bought at the airport in Oakland—James Baldwin's *Go Tell It on the Mountain*. When I was on the plane to Amsterdam I couldn't get excited by the book at all, but now that I'm in Ghana I can hardly stop reading. The story is about a black family in Harlem. The father is an unbearably religious and unloving storefront preacher. One of the sons is a proud, bitter rebel while the other is sensitive and thoughtful, trying to find himself. It's the second son, John, I identify with. He's grown up with religion ("Praise the Lords" and prayer meetings). John is pulled two ways—he's drawn to God's love but hates his father and everything he stands for. John finds a terrible contradiction in the lives of the "saints." Listen:

> *To walk in Jerusalem just like John. Tonight, his mind was awash with visions: nothing remained. He was ill with doubt and searching. He longed for a light that would teach him, forever and forever, and beyond all question the way to go; for a power that would bind him, forever and forever, and beyond all crying to the love of God. Or else he wishes to stand up now, and leave this tabernacle and never see these people any more. Fury and anguish filled him, unbearable, unanswerable; his mind was stretched to breaking. For it was time that filled his mind, time that was violent with the mysterious love of God. And his mind could not contain the terrible stretch of time that united twelve men fishing by the shores of Galilee, and black men weeping on their knees tonight, and he, a witness.*[1]

November 13

... I finished reading *Go Tell It on the Mountain* last night. I was unprepared for the ending. John was at church, at a prayer meeting. (Baldwin uses this prayer meeting as a literary device to provide flashbacks on all the main characters and to develop characters further—the meeting takes up about two-thirds of the book.) John is at the meeting, staring coldly at the "Jesus Saves" and "The wages of sin is death" signs, feeling like an observer, out of place, when suddenly something happens to him:

As now, in the sudden silence, she [John's mother] heard him [John] cry: not the cry of the child, new-born before the common light of earth; but the cry of the man-child, bestial, before the light that comes down from Heaven. She opened her eyes and stood straight up; all of the saints surrounded her; Gabriel [John's father] stood staring, struck rigid as a pillar in the temple. On the threshing-floor, in the center of the crying, singing saints, John lay astonished beneath the power of the Lord. [2]

And while this boy John lies on the floor he experiences a multitude of things—the emptiness and coldness of death, the hell of sin. He understands the love of God, and suddenly Jeremiah, John, Judas, Thomas, Peter, Moses, David, Stephen, Paul, all become real, and finally, Jesus:

Then John saw the Lord—for a moment only; and the darkness, for a moment only, was filled with a light he could not bear. Then, in a moment, he was set free; his tears sprang as from a fountain; his heart, like a fountain of waters, burst. Then he cried: "Oh, blessed Jesus! Oh, Lord Jesus! Take me through!" [3]

I never expected Baldwin to bring Johnny to the Lord.

I found tremendous power in the book. I expected much less from it—mere escapism for myself. I'm sure it wasn't coincidental that I picked this book at random from all the other books at the airport. It's one of God's ways of meeting my needs. Do you know what is quoted on the inside leaf of the book? Isaiah 40:31.

Love, Adwoa

December 5

Dear Kwadwo,

... I've begun receiving responses to the letter I sent to First Pres in Berkeley. I can hardly remember what I wrote and now people are telling me how I've blessed and encouraged them. Praise God. And yet is it always true that when we're in the middle of a situation it's hard to see God working? So often I feel like Peter. He told Jesus sincerely: "Even though they all fall away, I will not," and, "If I must die with you, I will not deny you." And then, when trouble arose, all of Peter's love and good intentions vanished. "I neither know nor understand what you mean." It's true that he loved Jesus deeply and had left all that he had to follow him; yet when night came and Jesus was suffering, Peter hadn't the courage to speak to him or accept the responsibility of their relationship. I can't explain why I feel that, like Peter, I'm denying my Lord. Yet I know that I do feel that.

I see the SU group here dwindling and struggling and I watch it in agony but seem helpless to lead the sheep Jesus has put in my charge. . . .

Love, Adwoa

November 28

Dear Kwadwo,

Yesterday our SU group attended a one-day rally at a secondary school in Accra. I eagerly anticipated it as a time for strengthening and building up our fellowship. It turned out to be a day of one disappointment after another without end.

We learned our lorry wouldn't be coming to take us to the school after all, so two of the SU leaders and I stood at the roadside for an hour trying to contract with one—no success. An SU member went to Tema and arranged for another one. It never came. Lunch wasn't ready on time. It was time to leave and I needed something from my room, but Afua had gone off to town without telling me and with my only key. I was annoyed. We finally booked another van only to arrive at the rally after the main speaker had finished and with most of us having to stand through the second half (a play by Korle Bu's Nurses Christian Fellowship). When it was time to leave, our lorry never showed. Two of the SU members disappeared. We finally returned after dinnertime with a lorry that overcharged us. Tired, hungry, confused, unhappy.

That didn't seem to be what our fellowship needed at all. The SU president was distressed and on the edge of tears as we prayed together for a few minutes. I felt discouraged and half began to wonder if I have a curse on me. Like King Midas everything I touch seems to freeze and die. I know I've committed everything into God's care, but wish I knew what to do. Pray with me.

Love, Adwoa

Journal Entry *December 8*

Fear not, for I have redeemed you;
    I have called you by name, you are mine. *(Is. 43:1)*
I am the LORD your God,
    who brought you up out of the land of Egypt.
Open your mouth wide and I will fill it. *(Ps. 81:10)*
For I, the LORD your God,
    hold your right hand;
It is I who say to you, "Fear not,
    I will help you." *(Is. 41:13)*

How do I find myself here in Ghana tonight with the mosquito coil burning and the students talking and someone's radio playing and the manager's sheep calling out to the night? Did I bring myself here? Did I control all these things? Oh Jesus, you know the answer. Who holds my hand when I'm too weary to rise from the dirt where I've fallen? ("I count everything as loss. . . .") Who comforts me when snow and family and hamburgers tempt me to self-pity? Who waits until my first empty prayer falls to the ground and my second, with unreal words, dies into the air and my third begins to fear and my fourth throws me on my knees and my fifth is desperate and then, finally, answers me when I can see his face shining with love because I've come to see myself as I am and stopped trying to lie to him? Do I need to tell you? Oh Jesus, to call you Lord from the lips outward is tasteless. To say, "My Father," in complacence is like drinking muddy water. But to fall on my knees and cry with my heart to you and to hear you answer is new life–is you–is peace–is rest.

Chapter 4
The First Term Ends

Dear Kwadwo,

I'm still trying to get a residence permit, and Ante Aku is still graciously contacting friends of hers to help me. Last week one of them took me to the Ministries and introduced me to some "big man." I'm still not sure whether he was a principal secretary or minister. Anyhow, during my private interview with him I briefly glimpsed how some people manage to by-pass all the bureaucratic red tape—and what the price is.

The honorable Dr. A. has a law degree from England. Sitting in his plush air-conditioned office I could see that he is intelligent and reasonably hard-working. When I explained my visa problem he was very kind—almost too kind. Then he took my arm to lead me over to one of the leather-cushioned chairs and began singing praises of Americans and America and making sophisticated advances toward me, including an invitation to travel with him to England sometime. I suspect his dignity, along with that of many other politicians, is somewhat tarnished. Despite my lack of responsiveness, he produced a letter that may aid me in obtaining a new visa. . . .

Love, Adwoa

[Coincidentally, in December this same minister traveled to California and was escorted around the Berkeley campus by my fiancé, the then president of the local association of Ghanaian students.]

October 26

Dear Kwadwo,

I returned to the Ministry of Internal Affairs again today—but did not see Dr. A. I must have been referred to seven different men while I was there, but it seems some progress is being made in the pursuit of the elusive visa. At least they now have a thick file on me! But what a way to learn patience.

Before returning to the school Afua and I stopped to buy some things we've wanted for a long time but couldn't afford—a mortar and pestle for making *fufu* and another mortar for pounding palm nuts.

When I picked up the two wooden mortars at Makola Market in Accra, those huge, perpetually-cheerful market women were shocked that ɔbroni had to carry them herself and reprimanded Afua. Of course the mortars are quite light, only weighing a few pounds each, but the idea itself initially appeared to shock the women. When I insisted on carrying them everyone in the marketplace was delighted. Row after row of the women in their stalls cheered and called out to me, flashing amused smiles—some of them even dancing a few steps to express their enjoyment. As usual my face reddened, but I managed to laugh too.

After we arrived home Afua and I prepared *fufu*. My

arms got tired pounding the boiled plantain and cassava in the mortar. I was sure I'd hit Afua as she turned the *fufu* between my irregular efforts. But the final product was well worth the energy expended.

Love, Adwoa

October 28

Dear Kwadwo,

... When the Ministry of Education decides to act, its members move with no forewarning. Several of them came to the headmaster's office unexpectedly today to gather "particulars" about my proposed class load, salary and so on. One man came to my classroom to observe my teaching. He arrived during an English language class. We had spent the entire period doing exercises on vowel sounds (for example, the difference between "fox" and "forks," "shot" and "short"). The students were so confused by my American English pronunciation that the lesson had been a fiasco. Fortunately, we were in the middle of correcting one of the exercises when he arrived and almost everyone knew what the correct sounds *should* be. The students were beautifully cooperative—all joking and playing stopped completely for the ten or so minutes he was present before class was dismissed and everyone went for breakfast.

It is good to know that the wheels of the Ministry of Education are turning, even if slowly.

Love, Adwoa

P.S. I'm convinced that none of my students or the SU members understood more than a few words of anything I said to them the first week I was here! I must be unconsciously picking up an accent though, because strangers have begun assuming I'm British.

November 13

Dear Kwadwo,

Afua is in my room resting on the bed. She had an attack of her "rheumatism" last night, and I took her to the hospital in Tema today. Poor girl, she suffered terribly but is much better tonight. Her illness frightens her. (It frightens me too.) I think she remembers when she was at that school in Asankragwa and had to leave because of her constant sickness. The doctor gave her some medicine, and I went to Accra this afternoon for some ointment, codeine and anti-malaria pills. I'll get her a hot water bottle soon, along with some socks. She returns to see the doctor on Friday.

Pray for your sister. . . .

Your other sister Ama was here this past weekend, and we all visited Ante Aku. On Friday morning Afua and I went to Adukrom and took Nɛnɛ [Kwadwo's grandmother] some provisions. She seemed glad to see us and sends you her greetings. I wore Afua's *kabba* and *ntama*, and Nɛnɛ was pleased to hear my stumbling Twi again. I enjoyed being there, and spending a day leisurely in your home.

As I grow closer to your family I begin to realize that I am accepting certain special responsibilities. Sunday night while Ama, Afua and I were in a lorry riding back to the school from Ante Aku's, I sensed this strongly. I guess I'm finally growing up? I'm happy to be young and healthy and strong but recognize that there's more to being a woman—a woman of God—than serving myself.

Love, Adwoa

November 22

Dear Kwadwo,

. . . Afua is sitting next to me laughing. She just picked up an agenda I wrote for our last board of governors meeting and saw that I had signed it as the "secretary." She eagerly looks forward to earning that title for herself. She is completely well now and continues to blossom. Every time someone comes to visit they remark how happy she is. She smiles much of the time. Her shyness is decreasing. She studies hard, and I'm sure she'll do well in her school exams. Her English is improving too. Finally, this term she made a decision to "know Jesus better," and it is taking root in her life.

Not until Afua was sick last week did I realize how dependent I am on her. I was forced to do simple things myself, like sweeping, cleaning, cooking, shopping. And I was surprised to find out how difficult I found these routine things, especially cooking. I'm trying to correct the situation now.

I wish you could have seen me learning to wash my laundry this morning. While we were laughing, the housemistress came to find out who was helping Afua. Seeing me, she smiled and watched, finally joining in our laughter. My knuckles are a little sore now, and I was sure my arms would give out before I finished. I've always let Afua wash before. I had scrubbed almost everything I have and was struggling to get them all wrung out, when I discovered that it needs to be done two or three times! I was dismayed but finally finished. I know that next time it'll be easier.

I also have a few blisters on my hands and feet. Those on my hands come from my feeble efforts at pounding *fufu* and those on my feet from some new leather sandals I bought in Accra (à la Ghana). I'm sure if you were here you'd laugh your precious laugh to see them. It is fulfilling to learn more self-reliance, and I'm glad I'm getting a little tougher. I praise the Lord for bringing me here.

Love, Adwoa

November 30

Dear Kwadwo,
It's time for evening studies and I'm in the typing room

supervising the commercial students who are also boarders. Only a handful of our fifteen-odd typewriters can be coaxed into working on any given day, so the students never get enough time to practice. That's why I've begun opening the room two nights a week for the boarding students and two afternoons a week for the day students who are taking typing. I don't have many minutes to write you while I'm here, though, because these ancient typewriters keep falling apart and I keep trying to fix them (not only are they in poor condition and exposed to the rain that often blows in through the opening between the tin roof and the "temporary" walls, the students also pound them to death) or one of the students who doesn't belong here sneaks in or someone has a question. I just gave our most advanced student a typing test (she had typing prior to coming to MODESCO, unlike everyone else, who has never studied it before)—thirty-three words per minute with fourteen errors! Still, a few of the students seem to be picking it up, bit by bit. . . .

Love, Adwoa

December 2

Dear Kwadwo,

I've been daydreaming about you, imagining the day we'll be together again. I try not to think about it too often because it sets me longing to be with you. I remember you a thousand different ways—silent, laughing, tired, happy, angry, hurt, meditative, busy, relaxing, sleeping. I remember you absorbed in your work in the lab, lying in the grass under the trees, sitting in church, cooking omelets at the co-op, camping with friends, playing table tennis, eating *fufu* with Kwamena. I remember us reading together, walking together, talking together, praying together. I remember you meeting me after work or my sitting on the granite steps of Hearst Mining Building singing slow, quiet songs and watching the Campanile till you met me.

September 5th I left Berkeley, and now that's three months ago. Yet it seems like only a few days ago that we were at Urbana and Paul Little was speaking about knowing God's will and being ready to sacrifice our preconceived ideas about our future. How little did I expect then what God had in store for me. I remember the day we had lunch together near the end of the convention, and sitting and talking with you and your roommate. I remember, too, when we went outside and played in the snow—you put snow in my face and on my neck. I met some of the Ghanaian Christians. So many memories. All these things seem as if they happened only yesterday, but I know they were just brief moments in time that have moved on never to return. Better days will come though—even better days.

Love, Adwoa

December 10

Dear Kwadwo,

I went to Ante Aku's last weekend. Instead of the usual forty-five or so minutes it took me about nine hours. I went to Accra Friday after classes and waited over two hours for the bus before someone informed the people in line that it had broken down. So I returned to Nungua. The next morning I went again and the bus came but broke down before we could leave. I waited about three hours. We were told that another bus would be coming. I finally rode to Achimota with some other people in a crowded taxi. I must be learning patience. I must!

Afua begins her first term exams today. She has been studying long and hard this term, and I'm sure she'll do well. Ama came last night to stay with us—she's still sleeping.

December 12

... I've kept this letter on my desk to finish and mail, but it's been difficult. Part of the problem is having Ama, Afua and me all staying in one small room. I don't want to go off by myself to write you or I'm unable to because of the girls and students in the room.

... I've just left my uncorrected exams at school. Ama and I are going to Accra—first to the Ministries, of course, and then to buy some material for dresses for the two girls. I've decided to stop everything and finish this letter so I can mail it as we go.

Love, Adwoa

December 14

Dear Kwadwo,

... When Ama and I went to the Ministries I discovered, not surprisingly, that I must return with a letter from the school before they'll extend my visitor's permit for another two months while they continue to process my application for a residence visa. I can see them playing around until the day I leave, but that's fine with me. I'm feeling pretty much at home at the Ministries now. While we were in Accra I bought the material for dresses for Ama and Afua and also some for the traditional African dress mom sent me money for....

Love, Adwoa

December 14

Dear Kwadwo,

I attended a tea party recently. Several of the women there were Ghanaian teachers at a preparatory school in Accra. Some whites had also been invited. Besides myself, there were three European women present, all married to West Africans.

I was delighted at the opportunity to question them about their experiences. One of the women (with long brown hair, oversized sunglasses, plenty of bright lipstick and eye shadow, lots of rings on her hands, and wearing an expensive-looking white pantsuit) was unapproachable. All I could discover is that she's a convinced spiritualist.

Of the other two women, one was leaving in a week for Europe. She had been here four years and has two children. I was told that her husband was on business abroad and that she and her family were flying to meet him to be together for Christmas. I accepted that and asked her numerous questions about how life has been here, explaining that I'm considering marrying a Ghanaian and that we've heard there are many problems in mixed marriages. She told me that when she and her husband came to Ghana they had had to struggle for many months before he could find a job. She advised that you be very sure you'll find work when you return. Other than that she was noncommittal. It wasn't until the next day that I learned another story. Her husband absconded some months ago, leaving her alone with the children. She's selling everything she has left to go home to her family.

I was most drawn to the third woman, probably because it was easiest for us to talk. She took a genuine interest in hearing about our plans and sharing what has happened to her. Her family adamantly disapproved of the marriage for about two years until they got used to it. Then they even got happy about it. She told me about the loneliness she feels since her husband is often away from home. She invited me to visit her and we exchanged addresses. She seems to have made the best adjustment to the Ghanaian way of life, though I suspect that she's an unhappy woman. She's been here ten years.

All of the women were nice, but I found it difficult to talk to them about things that really concern me. For example, I brought up an article in the paper a couple of weeks ago about teaching vernacular in the international schools. The writer was overly emotional and inaccurate in his accusations, but the point he was making was that these schools put so much stress on English and English textbooks that children grow up losing a basic part of their heritage and aren't able to communicate adequately in their mother tongue. The writer proposed using only vernacular textbooks for all subjects. This is impractical, but I understand his desire to be proud of his Africanness without having to bow to the West. It's that old familiar story. However, none of the other women at the party took this whole question seriously.

Also, I tried to talk with them about social problems that I think will continue to grow in the next few years. The young today are shown the fruits of the developed countries in terms of things—clothes, cars, stereos, soul music, dances, dress, lifestyle and so on. They think that whatever is new and different is superior, and thus they dream of leaving Ghana for the excitement of America. If that's not possible, they leave their hometowns like Adukrom for the glamorous big cities of Accra and Tema. Jobs are scarce and living expenses are high in these cities. They end up in a conflict that leaves both them and their families unhappy. The women didn't seem too interested in discussing that either.

Love, Adwoa

December 18

Dear Kwadwo,

Afua did very well on her exams and is well on her way to becoming a secretary. Her marks are mostly in the seventies, which is a good beginning in the Ghanaian system. Her English holds her back some, but as time passes it should become easier for her to understand and remember and then communicate the information presented to her. She continues to worry about her "rheumatism" though. It can become a problem at any time.

The Christmas holidays are almost here. Several of the students have asked me if I won't be spending them in America. I've explained that it would be a little difficult! Instead I'll leave tomorrow to join Kwaku at a five-day conference for Christian university students at Accra Academy. The girls will go there with me to say hello to Kwaku and then travel to Adukrom where I'll join them after the conference ends. Several people have already warned me against spending the night at your house in Adukrom. (They think the accommodations aren't suitable for *ɔbroni*.) I've had to be firm in explaining that Afua and I *are* going and that I'm not worried about the water problem or staying at the house. One of your uncles was going to find me a place to stay at Adukrom because he just didn't consider your parents' old house at all. Afua and I just laugh now.

Love, Adwoa

December 18

Dear Kwadwo,

I moved a desk and chair out onto the veranda of the girls' hostel and under the fluorescent light so I can correct exams tonight. Most students went home today. There is a stillness that makes me glad to be outside listening to the night sounds. The sheep are here, jumping around and climbing up the steps in front of me almost to the second floor. There are three eternal-looking mango trees peacefully breathing in the cool night air, too, and many palm trees. In the starlight the upraised fronds of the palm trees look like angels' wings poised to disappear up to heaven at any instant. Now the sheep have curled themselves against the ground and are radiating calmness. It must be almost morning because the cocks are beginning to crow—first from the right, then off to the left, and finally there's a chorus all around. I've wrapped a cloth around me to ward off the chill and the mosquitoes, and have been drinking tea all night from a thermos to keep me awake. . . .

One of the girls left her water bucket outside, and it looks like it belongs down on the ground all silver in the grass forever, with little frogs hopping in and out of its shadow. The dew and flowers have combined to fill the air with a delicate sweetness.

What did Gerard Manley Hopkins say?

". . . There lives the dearest freshness deep down things. . . ."

Well, it's about time for morning to slip up, so I must go back to my work. I hope this letter reaches you by Christmas. I think tonight is like the night Jesus was born.

Love, Adwoa

Part II
The Stranger's Eyes

ɔhɔho ani akɛseakɛse, nanso
onhu hwee.

*(The stranger's eyes are
very big from looking, but he
doesn't see anything.)*

Twi proverb

Chapter 5
A Vacation and a Coup

Dear Kwadwo,

I've come to Adukrom for Christmas. Kwaku and I spent last week at the Ghana Inter-University Christian Fellowship Conference at Accra Academy. It was a refreshing, stimulating time. One speaker talked about the slum conditions in a section of Accra and the attempts of Christians to help alleviate the associated social problems. I was also able to pick up some books and pamphlets to add to the growing collection I keep in my room at school as an informal SU library.

Yesterday we attended the Christmas Day service at church. It was, I believe, called a Thanksgiving Service, and lasted several hours. Much of the time was spent taking up a collection, followed by another and another. Everyone walked ceremoniously up to the plate to deposit their offerings. I felt extremely conspicuous going forward—

the long, green skirt and blouse outfit Afua sewed me for Christmas must have been a lovely contrast to my face. I only had a few coins to deposit. The elder, or whoever the man was counting the money, probably assumed I'd produce a large *cedi* note to drop into the plate.

Secretly, and irrationally, I was hoping to find an undemanding anonymity awaiting me in Adukrom. Of course that hasn't materialized. If anything I'm more of a curiosity here than at school. And naturally I feel unsure of myself much of the time. Good experience, huh? I'm most secure inside your parents' house. I imagine people wonder why I stay inside so much when everyone else only seems to go in to sleep.

I had lunch with your uncle Papa Dankwa too. He was kind to me and we had a delicious meal, but again I felt like I was on display and wanted to make a good impression. I do wish I could just relax and enjoy everything.

During my stay here Kwaku has been faithful about showing me around and introducing me to people, including one elderly lady whose feelings (expressed in Kyerepong) were, simply, "He wants to marry ɔbroni— humph! Let him take her to farm—then he'll see his mistake." She's quite right. I'd be useless with a machete and afraid at every step I'd run across a snake.

I've seen the school where your father was headmaster and heard stories about your mother's industriousness. Thinking about her teaching, bringing up her children, and raising poultry and goats reminds me of the "A good wife who can find" passage in Proverbs.

In the Presbyterian Church I thought about how many hours you must have been in the worn wooden pews. Even the way Kwaku teases me or laughs makes me think of you. Oh, how close you are to me at Adukrom. . . .

Love, Adwoa

January 2

Dear Kwadwo,

Today I met a man who just completed a doctorate in the states. He and his family seemed a bit pretentious (with his flashy American car and clothes). Nevertheless, I enjoyed our conversation which centered on their observations of some of America's problems, especially racism. Their children attended all-black schools, and they spoke about Chicago's south side as if they lived there. They told me about the "liberals" who invited them to come preach to their all-white congregations or people who were terribly concerned about the problems of Africa while oblivious to their own problems on the south side. They commented on other aspects of American life that had impressed them, including the political bosses of the Democratic Party in Chicago, the incredible violence in American cities, the drug problem.

While talking with them I remembered visiting a Ghanaian professor and his family in Berkeley once. I contrasted how nervous I was then with how I feel now, and I was glad I've been in Ghana. I recognize now that the problem isn't simply that my skin is white or that I'm from a developed country. . . .

Love, Adwoa

January 3

Dear Kwadwo,

I received Afua's term report today. She was first in her class!

It took Ama, Afua and me hours to clean our place today (we've returned from Adukrom). We spent the time leisurely working, laughing and talking. We looked at the gold jewelry that was your mother's, reminisced about our childhoods (I understand your father used to carry Ama on one shoulder to class when she was a baby and then use his free hand to write on the blackboard). Ama did some traditional dances and Afua sang songs to accompany her. The girls laughingly insisted on each receiving a child to care for, with one for Kwaku too.

It seems that even with all your relatives here, the girls were essentially left to fend for themselves after your parents died. I'm not being critical—as the title from a song that was once banned in Ghana says, there's "suffering in the land." Times aren't easy for people, and urbanization has brought many changes that make family obligations more and more difficult to fulfill.

That reminds me—I assume by now you've heard about the devaluation of the *cedi*? One dollar is now worth about 1.8 *cedis*. It's amazing—in two days prices have practically doubled—sugar has gone from thirty-five to sixty *pesewas* a bag. Something like a bottle of orange soda has jumped to two shillings from one. Someone tried to explain to me the implications of the devaluation and the rationale behind it as well—encouraging industry in Ghana and ultimate exportation, meeting your balance of payments deficit and things like that. All the average person in Ghana knows is that he or she is struggling as hard as ever and suddenly money has lost half its buying power. While the big men are struggling to get their share of the nice houses and cars and send their sons abroad, people really are suffering. How can anyone justify telling a hungry person to sacrifice when his only concern is with getting another car or stereo? An obvious question but conveniently ignored.

Incidentally, I've told the girls and Ante Aku that if you come to Ghana this summer we probably plan to be married. I haven't written my mother about it yet. I'm sure she won't be happy, but I know she agrees that the decision ultimately rests with us.

Love, Adwoa

January 6

Dear Kwadwo,

I can't sleep. I keep thinking about you. What a masochism there is about love: it hurts me to think about you, yet I'd rather suffer this pain than do anything else. . . .

Who is this man who has captured me so completely, whose very name makes my heart beat faster?

I've been recalling and reliving the years we've known each other and the gradual ripening of our sister-brotherliness into friendship and, then, into a marriage-directed love. Especially I was, like you, reminiscing about those beautiful days in early January last year. At first my feelings for you seem to have exploded upon me without any warning. But as I analyze our relationship I recognize in its growth the quiet, steady work of God's Holy Spirit.

Isn't it interesting that I should have asked you to help me with my anthro paper before I even knew you? Or that I happened to come to prayer meetings at your apartment where I happened to meet Vicki who happened to come live at Barrington and happened to be your friend when you happened to live half a block from our co-op? Interesting that I happened to come to spend part of the summer in Berkeley while you happened to be working there too.

I had the opportunity to see you in many different situations. Remember when I baked cookies at your apartment for geriatrics patients or the times I visited with you at the lit table. [A card table set up daily on campus by the local Inter-Varsity Christian Fellowship chapter to display and sell books on Christianity. The Sproul Plaza area in the late 1960s and early 1970s served as a marketplace of ideas. Tables were set up by religious, political and community service groups to provide forums for discussion of their particular ideology or philosophy. The Inter-Varsity booktable served as a ministry to both Christians and non-Christians.] I recall my growing respect as I watched you debating with campus skeptics. I was struck by your sensitivity and wisdom too. During lunches and dinners together I was impressed by the genuine interest you took in other people's lives. I saw you doing many good things without calling attention to yourself.

Somehow, at the Urbana conference God freed me to be obedient to him to do whatever he asked. That decision to take my hands off my life (meaning school, where I would live, whom I would marry) was the final step that led us to our exciting discovery of each other.

The last day of the conference, when we had lunch together, I was able just to enjoy your company. For the first time I knew I wouldn't say no to my feelings for you. Rather, I recognized that there was something very special about you to me. A few days later I began to understand why it had hurt me so deeply and why I had become so angry when my stepfather wouldn't allow you to come for dinner since you were black. It was because I loved you.

Adwoa

January 13

Dear Kwadwo,

We woke up at 5:30 A.M. this morning when someone staying at Ante Aku's rushed in to tell us there had been a coup. We sat around the radio until the news came on at 6:00 A.M. when Colonel Acheampong quietly announced that the military decided to remove Prime Minister Busia after they detected his "hypocrisy." All day since then the radio has played military music over and over, except for occasional announcements about what has happened.

Everything has been surprisingly peaceful and normal, though I am reminded of being in Berkeley during some of our upheavals. It seems unreal to wake up one morning and find that suddenly everything, from the constitution to the Parliament, has been dissolved. The newspapers have been filled with pro-Acheampong news, but there are rumors of possible counter-coups too. I went to the Ministries to try to discover how the coup will affect my visa (right now I don't have one). There are plenty of scared big men around.

The new government is called the National Redemption Council (NRC), and the Opposition Party is just as unwelcome as the Progress Party now. Tonight they announced on the news that Black Star Square has had its name changed to Independence Square or something like that. The names of the Black Star steamship lines and Black Star team are also to be changed. Interesting reforms.

The implications of military rule don't appear to bother most people much at all. All my classes on U.S. government and the balance of power make it seem an unattractive alternative. However, I've heard people say, "We've given the brilliant theorists and moralists (that is, the Busia government) a chance, and what have they done?" The biggest complaint ordinary people have is that the big men making the theories and telling people to suffer haven't been doing any suffering themselves. People see the ministers' big houses and expensive cars, and then they hear how they're to sacrifice. Even though the people don't know economics, they know something's wrong. (That's not to deny that those same people would just love their own big houses and cars if there was any way that they could get them.)

I understand that Ghana is the only African country where the military ever handed over power to civilians. Now that has changed. This makes the third coup here since independence, doesn't it? Can you tell me more about coups? Aren't they common in South America? Why do some countries like India never experience them?

Incidentally, I'm sure my mother has heard something about the coup and is worried. Please reassure her—tell her that I'm fine and temporarily staying at Ante Aku's.

Love, Adwoa

Journal Entry *January 13*

I've started to be afraid again. The newness and excitement of coming to Ghana, getting a job, eating fufu, *wearing* ntama *and* kabba, *and being at Adukrom have become things that—how do I say it?—no longer impress me now that I've done them. The undying enthusiasm and determination that have plunged me into new and newer experiences have lost their original freshness. I've recognized some of the demands made on me by living in Ghana, and I've wondered if I'm a fool. Every new story about unhappy mixed marriages makes me ask, Are we so different?*

When I'm sick there'll be no mother to run to and no family (meaning my own sisters and brothers) to be with; maybe never even to see again before I die. My effectiveness as a social worker will be crippled by my inability to speak any vernacular languages easily and by the fact that I'm not, and never will be, a Ghanaian by birth. There will always be a battle for acceptance into people's inner circles. I can't live my life forever in an ivory-towered university world. The economic, political, agricultural and social problems all scare me because they're so big. I get tired of not really belonging.

At Legon I felt it again today. I want to be humble and lead a simple life, but my experiences at school and home have given me some interests that are hard to share with many people. Even dear Ante Aku doesn't think it's necessary for me to go to graduate school. . . . The girls were laughing at a ballet on the TV tonight. It was just funny to them to see something like that. I don't blame them—for them it was funny, but it hurt me a little. It's hard when the clothes I like aren't acceptable for "Christians" and some of the music I enjoy is thought bad too.

It's hard to take the things I've been taught to do and be since I was a little girl and suddenly put that all behind me. Tonight I couldn't eat all my dinner. . . .

I know the danger of homesickness and remembering only the good things I left behind, like Lot's wife. God, you know my aching heart—give me your grace.

January 14

Dear Kwadwo,

... I went to Legon yesterday with Ante Aku to visit her class at the primary school (the coup didn't stop business as usual, it seems) and also to see where a friend works at the Ghana Commercial Bank. The bank was full of Americans rushing to exchange their dollars before the devaluation of the *cedi* is canceled, as everyone assumes it will be. This way they double their money at Ghana's expense.

I then stopped at the University library and spent some time looking through a book on community development in Ghana. It discussed field workers in the rural parts of Ghana and described things like mass literacy campaigns and starting young farmers' clubs. The writer was highly concerned about making agriculture a viable option for the young, educated male. How often I've heard that story. The second book I skimmed was related. It was a study on migration from villages to towns. I'm especially interested in urbanization and the changes it brings. I see the fascination with the bright lights and the bars of Accra in the faces of my own students. ...

Love, Adwoa

January 18

Dear Kwadwo,

I've been thinking and praying about our wedding. While I'd like to dispense with the whole ceremony and quietly exchange vows in the presence of a minister and Kwaku, Ama and Afua, something inside me says that a wedding should also be a time of joyful celebration with others. The problem here is knowing who to ask and who not to. Afua told me frankly last night that she doesn't want us to marry in Ghana. She realizes you and I don't have any money. If word gets around that we married here and didn't invite certain friends and relatives, they will be very hurt and insulted. It's simple on my side since I imagine none of my family would be able to be present. What about your family?

Ante Aku has been like a mother, but your sisters' guardian is still a stranger. Friends like Kwamena or Franklin would be easy to invite, and I know they wouldn't expect more from us than we could give. It's difficult for me because I'm unsure how far to go in any one direction. I know I'll be fortunate to find money to live through the summer —I won't be paid by the school. To think about the expenses of a wedding when I have barely enough money to pay for my ticket home seems absurd. Still, I want our wedding to be something to remember, and I believe nothing is impossible with God.

At any rate, the wedding will be simple but not plain. We'll supply the joy freely. Do share your thoughts.

Love, Adwoa

Chapter **6**
Back to School

Journal Entry *January 21*

I just returned from Korle Bu. Afua was operated on today. It's her leg again. We'd been trying to arrange the operation since late December. We must've gone to Korle Bu thirty times trying to set a date.

In Ghana there are three ways to get something done. One, you get a relative or influential friend into a strategic position, and you sail through over everyone else's head. Two, you pull out a few cedis and wave them under someone's nose ("scratch his throat," as they say here). Three, you resign yourself to the normal channels and prepare to wait. Even though you mentally reject the first two alternatives, the third becomes less appealing when someone you love is suffering and you wait days to see a doctor who prescribes some tests that take weeks and then come to find the tests haven't been finished because someone didn't bother to follow through and they have to be repeated (while this person is still suffering) and then you find the first doctor forgot to assign the most important test and you wait for the results, and come, and come again and then are admitted to a ward and then told you have to wait until a bed is ready and that may take months because many people are trying for every bed that empties and you check and check and receive incomplete and incorrect information and finally are told to come and bring your things and then sent away because you need three pints of blood donated . . . and on and on and on. And Korle Bu is called the best hospital in Ghana.

It's all right to wait three or four hours for a bus. It's all right to wait five months for a residential permit. But to watch Afua suffer tears me apart. I know, Lord, that you've got the whole world in your hands. Help me to trust you.

January 22

Ma adwo, me dɔ fo pa [Good evening, my love],

. . . Afua is now recovering from yesterday's operation, and will probably be on the ward for several weeks while the bone heals. However, some friends at the medical school told me her operation was probably just to remove dead bone and may not be especially helpful. Still, Afua's doctor told her yesterday that he'll refer her to another doctor at Korle Bu who knows a lot about sickle cells.

I must admit, my confidence is being restored in the staff at the hospital. Once you finally get in, everything changes from when you're just looking in from the outside. . . .

Love, Adwoa

January 24

Dear Kwadwo,

I'm learning to plan my days and set priorities. This morning I was finishing some work before the SU meeting when some senior students ran into my room before the Sunday worship service to ask me to lead it. They had the responsibility to prepare for it, but somehow no one had been assigned to it. Last term I would have felt compelled to drop my plans and rush off with them ("Here am I, send me!"), trusting the Holy Spirit to work everything out. However, my experiences last term convinced me that not only am I not indispensable, I'm not to be in bondage to other people's demands. I'm to listen to the Holy Spirit and decide what it means to be obedient to Jesus. This morning that meant declining to preach and explaining why.

Friday night I faced a similar situation: I returned from Korle Bu about 8:30 P.M. I hadn't eaten, I had some letters to write and I was tired. As I walked onto the compound I passed the mango tree where a woman named Christiana sells bread and oranges to the students. Standing next to her was the housemaster (the spiritualist I wrote you about). I sat down on a bench next to Christiana to talk with them, and the first thing the housemaster said to me was, "I was waiting for you. God brought you here." I saw he was dressed up for church and could smell talcum powder (or "lavender," as the girls say) radiating from him. He said I should go to church with him. Last term if he had said that I would have impulsively felt I should go with him, partly to keep from hurting his feelings and partly to see if God actually had something to teach me. Instead, I thought a minute and then honestly told him I couldn't go until next Thursday or Friday evening. Afterwards I relaxed a few minutes with Christiana and went in to finish my work. Again, I didn't let the housemaster's demands destroy the freedom Christ gives me.

Most importantly, as I learn to move within a more disciplined and structured framework, God is blessing the work with the SU. I've learned that my purpose is not to *lead* the group at the meetings but rather to pray for, exhort and guide the students, and to concentrate on working with a small executive committee composed of the more mature Christians. The result is that our program is already well-organized. There is an enthusiasm and sense of purpose that was totally missing last term.

Also, God has answered my prayer for deeper fellowship and support with the SU work. Harry, a Christian who was in Form 5 at the school last year, has just returned here to teach art.

Love, Adwoa

January 26

Dear Kwadwo,

... It's been so long since I've touched you, since we stood together at the airport. Remember the red dress and scarf my mom sewed for me as a going away gift? I made you close your eyes while I tied the scarf around my hair. I can still see the approval and happiness on your face and hear your delighted laugh as you said it was "typically African." I have it on now, but the cloth is faded and the bright blue flowers against the red have turned almost white in parts. That's another reminder that over four months have passed since you whispered "Christ be with you" in the crowd as I headed to the plane at the Oakland airport. ...

I've begun weekly current affairs times in my classes. The students enjoy making oral presentations, but repeatedly insist on clipping jokes or sports items from the newspapers rather than political, social or economic events. Today, after my first period class the students' master didn't come, so I stayed through the second period too. The students asked me more questions about life in the United States: "Do mad (that is, crazy) people just go around the towns dirty and in rags like here?" "Do you buy food and things outside in the market like here?" "Do you have Coca Cola?" I spent a long time trying to explain the difference between *communal* and *nuclear* families. Some of them told me it was very bad that I've never even met my mother's mother. I tried explaining to them that we have to learn not to always say that it's bad—just that it's different.

Love, Adwoa

P.S. Afua will be discharged from Korle Bu in a few days.

Over the months I moved past my original naiveté regarding MODESCO. It was one of the "mushroom" schools springing up overnight throughout Ghana. The survival of these schools depended on the popularity of education and the belief that it was the key to success. Many parents of MODESCO students were farmers or fishermen who scrimped to save up enough cash to pay their children's tuition and fees at secondary school. As the school had basically no entrance requirements and almost no educational standard, the parents' dreams were largely illusions. Most students had scored too low on the standard entrance exam to qualify to enter a government-supported secondary school. Unless they could transfer to a government school before they reached the upper forms, they had almost no chance of going on to the advanced level preparation necessary to compete for entrance at one of the three Ghanaian universities. I learned that for many of the oldest students a MODESCO was the only place they could go through the motions of completing their fourth or fifth years.

January 28

Dear Kwadwo,

I now recognize two of MODESCO's weakest points. The headmaster is pleasant but is weak and unwilling (or unable) to command the respect of the students. Also, there are rumors that he's too friendly with some of his female students, which makes discipline even more impossible. Second, the boys' housemaster is simply incompetent. He has absolutely no respect among the students and, consequently, no control over them. Lights out, evening studies and inspection have all become one big joke to the boys. When I first came here I lamented the harshness shown toward the students. I've learned that most of that is an empty show and, most importantly, inconsistent. The girls' housemistress is able to handle the girls much better. She simply treats them the way their own mothers would: You're to keep your room neat, bathe when it's time to bathe, sleep when it's time to sleep and so on. I'm sure the girls have a healthy respect for her.

Still, unless the manager does something about the house and headmasters, the school may not survive. For example, last term almost all the Form 5 students refused three times to take their final exams. They knew they would fail and didn't want to lose face since the results would be posted outside the administration building. Consequently, the headmaster announced that as a result of last term's behavior, the Form 5 students involved would not return. He was supported completely by the teachers who had taught the students, the board of governors, and the boys' housemaster and girls' housemistress. The students who had been dismissed and told they would not be readmitted under any circumstances continued to come and beg to be readmitted. He began letting a few in. Soon almost everyone had returned, except for three students who had been recommended for dismissal on the basis of inappropriate behavior before this even happened.

Don't think students in Forms 1 through 4 don't realize that the Form 5 students are winning over the administration. ("They're back, after all.") The Form 5 students are already causing problems. They're willing to be humble and repentant to the administration's face, but now that they're back in they're angry and bitter. They're no longer allowed to be prefects. They've lost their powers and they've lost face. Now they only want to sabotage the school. To crown everything, the headmaster has just decided to readmit the three boys he had unconditionally declared would not be allowed to return. . . .

Love, Adwoa

February 5

Dear Kwadwo,

. . . Last week the housemistress went away for a few days and left me in control of the girls' boarding house. Since there are no senior prefects now that means a lot of responsibility for a novice like me. I understand from one of the students that the older girls were planning what they could do for some excitement while I was in charge. I played right into their hands.

The girls were good all day Wednesday, during siesta time and during evening studies. Downstairs in the dormitories there was complete silence after lights out. I was relieved but didn't leave well enough alone. I went to the upstairs dorms and caught the older girls laughing and talking. After reprimanding them and taking down some of their names I went back to my room. Later I decided to check upstairs one last time. I felt committed—against my will and nature—to see this responsibility through.

Upstairs I saw lights still on in some of the dorms and heard laughter. As I started down the corridor the girls spotted me, and the doors were locked and total silence descended. I pounded on one of the doors until a girl sleepily opened it. When I turned the light on, it was to see every single girl, ostensibly, sleeping. I "woke" each one and announced the entire dorm would be reported to the office the next day. They were all indignant, swearing they'd been sleeping. But I told them to turn the light out and left. I didn't return to my room, though. I went to the end of the corridor, turned right and stood by the window waiting to see if they'd stay quiet. They called to me several times to see if I were still there. When they were sure I was gone, they burst into loud laughter. I heard them making fun of me in Ga, saying my name and imitating the way I talk. One dorm was particularly loud. By now I was getting very angry that they were taking everything as a joke. My own sense of humor evaporated.

I went to the dorm and stood outside listening to the voices but couldn't distinguish them because I didn't know those girls. When I decided I'd given them enough time to settle down, I banged on the door so hard it shook. You would have thought everyone inside suddenly died. I told the girls to open the door, that I'd been listening to them for ten minutes. No answer. I even kicked the door while I pounded on it. No answer. (In retrospect, I don't know how they could keep from laughing, unless they were scared.) I pushed the door open a few inches even though a trunk blocked it, turned the light in the room on and kept knocking. No answer. If I'd been angry before I was furious now. I never knew such a strong emotion could take hold of me like that. They still refused to answer. I warned them again and said if they wouldn't open the door I'd go get the housemaster to force it open. They still didn't respond so I started down the hall.

(I was already exhausted that night. I was up during the previous night with a girl suffering from malaria and an ulcer. All Wednesday I'd had classes and girls coming and going, and an evening meeting with the SU executive. I just wanted to sleep in peace. That partly explains, though doesn't excuse, my behavior.)

As I walked away I calmed down and realized that if I just stayed there, sooner or later they'd have to open the door. I went back and began talking to them again, saying that they didn't have to open it since their names were all written on it. Then I read the names one by one and started writing them in my notebook. Inside, they all knew what I was doing. When I discovered that two of the girls were Form 5 girls I repeated their names and said I was surprised at them and surely wouldn't forget them—they should know better.

When I said that, one of them, Mary, flew to the door, tore it open and began screaming at me, "What is this? Form 5, Form 5, Form 5—always picking on the Form 5 students." She said she'd been sleeping soundly to suddenly hear me shouting, "Mary, Mary, Mary, I'm sending the Form 5 students to the office." She ran out of the room with the rest of the girls, shouting. She woke up the students in the other dorms downstairs and many of them came out to see what was happening.

I listened to her shouting in Ga and asked some of the girls if she was abusing me. They admitted she was and advised me to just go to my room and she'd quiet down. Fancy that. If I'll go to my room, lock my door and go to sleep, one of the students (even if she's probably older as well as twice as big as I am) will do me the favor of quieting down after she's roused the whole dorm, disobeyed me and abused me. I was enraged! I told the other girls that none of the students tell the mistress what she can and cannot do and when to go to her room. Rather it works the other way around. Then I sent them all back to sleep and went upstairs to Mary's dorm to settle the confrontation.

As I went up I saw that someone had just torn the notices I'd posted that afternoon, crumpled them viciously and thrown them on the floor—I'm sure it was Mary. I went out to the veranda, called the two seniors and spoke to them privately. I explained that I wasn't separating them out from the rest of the group, that all were to be punished, and that rather than *me* disgracing Mary, she'd disgraced herself. I agreed to let the housemistress decide their punishment and sent them to bed.

I can't tell you how happy I was that the housemistress returned here Thursday night before lights out.

Love, Adwoa

January 31

Dear Kwadwo,

I just returned from an evening with two American missionaries. They cooked a special American dinner for me—complete with homemade cookies. We had a good time together. I'm afraid I was a bit judgmental the last time we met. I overreacted when I saw that their house looked like they were still living in America, and I had cultural reactions when I heard the name of the Bible college their child attends. However, I was able to talk with them about many things—especially intermarriage.

Rev. K. does some marital counseling (often with African men trying to understand their foreign wives or white wives trying to save their marriages). He believes that the marriages, Christian or not, are very often unsuccessful whether the couple stays together or not. He expressed a special concern regarding the cultural pressures ("You don't marry a person. You marry a culture.") that have so often destroyed marriages—demands that the relatives make, whether it means traditional customs regarding funerals or sex. "Responsibilities" to the extended family ("helping") means that there may be aunts, uncles, cousins, nieces, brothers, sisters, nephews and others who demand assistance from one spouse to the extent that it becomes difficult to support his/her own nuclear family.

Both Rev. and Mrs. K. felt that to live with you or come to know you in the American culture would be completely different from knowing you in Ghana. We discussed differing ideas regarding monogamy, expressions of affection and communication between husband and wife. They stated their conviction that no matter how ethical the person, it's practically impossible to overcome the cultural pressures. They observed that some companies in Africa have discovered that the most appropriate solution is for the husband and wife to live neither in her home country nor in his.

Love, Adwoa

February 6

Dear Kwadwo,

Yesterday I received a letter from Kwaku containing some tracts. During the Christmas holidays Afua had filled out a coupon in Rev. Don Stewart's *Miracle Magazine* asking for prayers for healing, and Kwaku had sent it in. The group, known as A. A. Allen Revivals, Inc., sent a collection of tracts including "How to Receive the Holy Ghost," "How to Receive and Keep Your Deliverance" and "A Miniature Handkerchief for You" (a small piece of cloth that, when prayed with and received in faith, *will* heal you). Kwaku wrote that he believes God will heal Afua miraculously. He asked me to study the tracts, explain them to her and pray with her for healing. I was going to see Afua that very afternoon and I felt trapped.

My immediate reaction was unbelief, and yet I knew that Afua has the right to ask God to heal her. I felt that if someone else could talk to her about these things it would be much better. I knew my skepticism would prevent anything from happening.

I shot up a quick prayer for wisdom. Then I took my NEB and RSV translations of the Bible, began to look up the Scripture alluded to in the tracts and to consider statements like, "You can make your own preparation that will guarantee perfect results," or "He believes it is done [that is, that God has healed him] because GOD SAYS SO: 'With his stripes WE ARE HEALED.' " Isaiah wasn't talking about faith healing, and I felt like the fantastic Reverend is just plain taking things out of context. Yet, the Bible does clearly show that God can and did heal people in ways not acknowledged (or understood) by modern scientific medicine.

Other references that left me unconvinced as "proof" that God will heal "every person" who asks him were: a part of Deuteronomy 7:15 ("The LORD will take away from you ALL SICKNESS"); or "Now is the acceptable time; behold now is the day of salvation" (2 Cor. 6:2), or "Beloved, I wish above all things that thou mayest prosper and be in health, even as thy soul prospereth" (3 Jn. 2, AV). Basically, Stewart says that God's Word can't lie, so as soon as you realize that it's God's will to heal everyone, you're ready to be prayed for. After you pray, you're to believe that you're healed, no matter whether anything seems different or not. Rev. Stewart has written a book, too, called *God's Guarantee to Heal You.*

As I was praying over these things I unexpectedly had a visitor from Korle Bu Medical School. Well, here was a medical student and a Christian! We talked for hours, and I didn't even get around to asking my question until just as we both left for Korle Bu—he was going home and I was on my way to see Afua. As we rode together in the tro-tro discussing faith healing, he said, "If you're really interested, there's a Christian doctor at Korle Bu who's going to talk about these things to some of the medical students tonight." I asked who it was and he said, "Dr. Konotey-Ahulu." I'd often heard about this man. Last week when I was discussing intercultural marriage with some American missionaries, they spoke of him and his British wife as the one intercultural couple they could think of with a successful marriage. Also, he is to be the speaker at an SU rally next week. I decided to stay at Korle Bu to hear him.

Dr. Konotey-Ahulu spoke quietly but gave his talk with a good sense of humor. He chose incidents from his own experience to illustrate what he said. He also brought reprints of an article he published in the *British Medical Journal* in 1969 on the question of phenomena that medicine can't explain, drawing again on his own personal experience. Though he has experienced healing personally, he is sensitive to the fact that God doesn't heal everyone—if that were the case, no one would ever die, or at least some never would.

He described the scene at a healing meeting he attended in Ghana: hundreds of diseased people—blind, crippled,

and others were all present—waiting to be healed. Up in
front was a big sign proclaiming "Christ Is the Answer."
Just before the prayer for healing, all the crutches, wheel-
chairs and other paraphernalia were sent to the front to
make a huge pile. After the prayer maybe eighteen people
were healed, some genuine healing miracles. But not everyone was healed. He described how amid all the joy and jubi-
lation he cried as he watched a young girl, crippled by polio,
trying to crawl away on all fours. Her crutches were down in
the pile, but there was no healing for her as people stepped
over and around her. "Is Christ the answer for her?" he
asked one of the evangelist's assistants and received the
callous explanation, "She couldn't reach out to God
enough." Dr. Konotey-Ahulu referred to the passage in
Matthew's Gospel where at the final judgment Jesus will say
to some very surprised people, "I never knew you; depart
from me," even though they can claim many miracles and
healings. He asked, "What about all those who weren't
healed and so because of a wrong doctrine lost their faith,
those who received neither hope nor comfort in their pain
because they couldn't 'reach out to God enough'? Our God
reaches down to us because we can *never* reach out to him
enough."

Love Adwoa

February 12

Dear Kwadwo,

I brought Afua back with me yesterday afternoon. She'll
go to Korle Bu every three days to have her leg dressed and
every three weeks to see Dr. Konotey-Ahulu. It turned
out *he* was the doctor whose expertise is on sickle cell
anemia. . . .

We went to the SU rally today. Remember the comedy
of errors I told you about last term? Everything was completely reversed today. While our bus was delayed over an

hour in arriving, it appears that the delay was intended to allow four of our day students to meet us and go with us. If we'd gone earlier they would have been left behind. We arrived at the rally before it started this time and returned promptly afterwards. God is so close to us this term. . . .

We didn't have classes last Friday. Several teachers here have been urging the administration to take firmer action against the students who are causing problems in the school. As a result, the staff met last Friday and decided to dismiss two students and suspend two others, including the Form 5 girl who threatened to beat me while the housemistress was away. She practically caused another riot last week, beat up her sister (also a student here) and even came to blows with the headmaster on Friday when she refused to leave the school compound. He tried to take her by the hand and she swung at him. She finally left, only to hurl abuse and accusations of witchcraft at the housemistress just outside the school grounds. . . .

Love, Adwoa

February 20

Dear Kwadwo,

Last Saturday was Afua's birthday, and we celebrated with *abɛnkwan* (palmnut soup) and *fufu*, followed by a small cake. I gave her a bookbag from you and me. She's eighteen now and feels like she's growing old too fast.

. . .Last time she went to Korle Bu the nurses told her that her operation has healed, so now she only needs to go to the hospital about once a month to see Dr. Konotey-Ahulu about her sickle cells. She is working hard at school, trying to make up the time she lost. She has been growing in her faith as well. . . .

Love, Adwoa

February 24

Dear Kwadwo,

I became ill at the end of last term and the doctor told me I needed to rest, so I decided to take things easier this term. Unfortunately, circumstances haven't allowed me to do that. The housemistress is still feeling sick and rundown and has left the school again, meaning the girls continue to be in my charge. Also, the assistant headmaster has been sick and absent over a week now, which means there's been no one to help me in the office. I feel like too many things are being dropped on me too quickly, yet I have no choice but to accept these responsibilities. Pray for me. . . .

I had planned to visit Ante Aku over the midterm break, but since the housemistress was away and the housemaster left too, I had to remain. I'm probably the least qualified person for the job of supervision: I'm too young and inexperienced, and I don't know enough about Ghanaian culture to know how to handle some things that arise. One evening over the midterm holidays I was up all night trying to locate three girls who ran off and stayed away until five the next morning. Another evening I found six girls sleeping together in three beds—one of the girls is an executive member of the SU. When I questioned them about *why* they were afraid to sleep alone they all said "because of ghosts." How could I answer them? Another night one of my Form 2 girls came to tell me she was afraid to sleep in her bed because the girl who slept above her last term (and who didn't return to school this term) died in childbirth last Wednesday. It was a genuine crisis for this girl.

. . . I've been learning some practical first aid—what to do in case of "rheumatism," fever, colds, headaches and other ailments. Those four are the most common, along with stomachache. Usually that means menstruation and the girls are having cramps, though sometimes it means diarrhea. I'm getting to know the girls better. I wonder what kind of a mother I'll make?

By the way, I realized the obvious a few days ago—that I've been trying to hide my insecurity behind a façade of strictness. I've been afraid I'll lose control of the students, so I've tried to act strict and disciplined (as I did the other night with Mary), ostensibly wanting them to behave so they'll learn better. Actually, I've been irritated with and hurt by them too. I'm sure I haven't fooled anyone by my show of "strength." I realize now that I've been confusing love and weakness. Pray for me that I learn to be patient and kind without resentment or irritation and that the qualities spoken of in 1 Corinthians 13 and the fruit of the Spirit in Galatians 5 become manifested in me. Unless they do, all my teaching is useless.

Love, Adwoa

Chapter **7**
Day by Day

February 20

Dear Kwadwo,

... I wish I'd thought up a good answer to why I continue to say I want to marry you despite all the difficulties that have been so freely prophesied for us. I do believe there are very real problems we'll have to confront, and I don't expect we'll find it easy to always agree. However, the development of our relationship over the years (especially over the last year), the way God cleared the way for me to come to Ghana and meet your family, the chance to count the cost before we begin building our life together, my inner conviction that we're moving along the proper path, the growth that's come about in our lives as a result of the few steps we've already taken, all contribute to my desire to become your wife.

Love, Adwoa

February 24

Dear Kwadwo,

The other night the housemistress spoke to me about our possible marriage. She had plenty of unhappy marriages as resource material to illustrate her points. One exception was a European woman married to a Ghanaian. The housemistress knew her, I think, from Keta and described her as, "So sensible—she puts on cloth, lives in her husband's town and is happy." Most of the stories weren't happy—wives falling into "temptation" when Europeans came around or husbands running around with Ghanaian women.

One problem the housemistress touched on was that when things begin to go wrong the Ghanaian will receive the sympathy of his or her family. The spouse might be told, "Who asked you to marry a foreigner?" "We tried to tell you this would happen," and so on. Family and friends might well urge the termination of the relationship. She also reminded me that my blood relations, my family, would be far away and thus unable to give me support. In addition they might continue to try to undermine the marriage by encouraging me to give it up, admit I made a mistake and come home before I have children. She warned that even some of the family members I've come to know and love here may simply decide that *I've* changed and blame me when there are difficulties.

Again we discussed the different family structure. For example, she said that the depression and loneliness a European feels is much deeper than that of Ghanaians. In Ghana, when something goes wrong, you immediately run to sister, brother, aunt, uncle, mother, father, grandmother or cousin. That person will sit on the case to decide things and try to help. Also, when the husband goes "on trek" (away on business) and leaves the woman behind, she has her family around to keep her company. A European, however, usually fights things out alone, especially if she's come to another country to live. People don't feel free to rush to her aid.

The housemistress stressed how important good health is, partly because health affects your whole being and perspective on life. She also said that the whites who marry Ghanaians and return here to live are often sympathetically viewed as "Your Innocent Mistake."

On the other hand the housemistress firmly believed that I can't compare myself to others who came to Ghana without knowing much about what to expect. She feels that, from what she's seen of Kwaku and Afua, I don't have to worry about your family. She thinks if you're like them, you're sure to be sober, balanced, honest, loyal and so on.

In fact, she said that if I should decide not to come back to Ghana with you, she wouldn't have any sympathy for me. Rather, all her sympathy would go to you, my husband-to-be.

Love, Adwoa

February 24

Dear Kwadwo,

Today I began to read *Hidden Art.* I smiled to read Edith Schaeffer's description of the early years of her marriage (during the depression era when neither money nor jobs were to be found). Reading about how she and her husband creatively transformed the places they stayed at touched and even inspired me. When she talked about the flowers they planted, I thought of the bright blue-purple morning-glories with rich leaves that cheer me every morning outside my window.

I laughed when I read how she and her husband used their imagination and talents to create their own furniture, remembering the evening you and I spent carting the throwaways from the alley behind Alko Office Supply, and how you broke the glass in the door trying to bring one of the wooden display cases into the co-op. Listening to her talk about the importance of music in every home made me remember one Sunday afternoon when you were playing the piano in the church lounge and some of us were singing with you. You told me how amazed you were that you decided to marry someone who couldn't sing. I read about making candles and thought how much I like them, remembering too the picture I painted for you one night of one of mine burning.

Thank you for sending me the book. On every page I find things I can relate to our experiences together, and it fills me with a kind of growing excitement, thinking about the possibilities in a Christian home. You know, sometimes we spend so much time anticipating our intercultural difficulties that we forget the blessings that God can give us. I want a home that will be a place where we'll want to come, a place to know love and beauty and joy and quiet and laughter, a place where our brothers and sisters of all races can come and belong, a place to bring people freely. It's nice to dream—I dream of a place that will make God's love and kingdom more real and more believable to those who come. And somehow, a place where the world's hectic, pressing, racing pace will draw away to leave us in peace. We'll have a lifetime together to create it.

Love, Adwoa

March 1

Dear Kwadwo,

My experiences in Ghana are helping me overcome the feelings of inferiority that bottled me up before when I met black women. Remember how I felt it was difficult for me to develop genuine, spontaneous friendships with black Americans in my college classes? How I often ended up trying too hard.

It's true, though, that I haven't made any close friends in Ghana who are women. It's not that I haven't had any contact with women but more that the friendships that develop between me and others are among men. Most of your friends I've met are men, and almost all the teachers and administrators at the school are men too. The fact that Harry is here results in my needs for fellowship being met by him rather than a woman. We see each other daily, pray together, share together and often eat together. Though I spend time with Afua and the other girls, I feel older and separated from them. Even in the SU group I know the boys best because they are the active leaders.

More than this being an acute problem, it is something I periodically ponder and then forget. Is it just circumstances that have caused this situation . . . or is it possible that rather than me finding Ghanaian women threatening, maybe they find me threatening? . . .

Love, Adwoa

March 2

Dear Kwadwo,
Tonight after fixing my meal I went to the roof to eat. Then I came downstairs and helped Afua with her economics. Later I went to talk with Christiana. Last week she saw me wearing a long dress and half-seriously asked me to give it to her: "Oh, I beg you!" Last night (it was cold) she saw me sitting on our veranda and came over to admire my sweater. She said she was cold because she didn't have one and her little boy didn't either. My instinctive reaction was that she assumed I'm rich and could give her anything she asked for since I'm an American. I told her I was sorry, I only had two. Later that night I began to think—didn't Jesus say if we have two shirts we should give one away? I remembered Christ saying things about going the extra mile and giving to those who ask from you. I thought, "It's true that I have two and she doesn't have any. And she sits outside all day and into the night selling her oranges and

small loaves of teabread." It seemed that obedience to Jesus' word demanded, against my natural desires, that I should give her one of the sweaters. I did so this evening.

Love, Adwoa

February 29

Dear Kwadwo,

Last night despite all my will power I fell asleep before the girls were to go to bed. There was no one to send them to sleep or to check them on their noise. I woke up with a start at about 5:00 A.M., still tired. When I realized it was morning I rolled out of bed onto my knees and prayed that God would take away my responsibilities in the boarding house. I felt something had to be done. I prayed for wisdom and then did what I wanted to anyhow—I wrote a letter to the headmaster asking to be relieved of duties in the boarding house, to be relieved of my classes and to be given a full-time job in the office and library, establishing them properly and setting up a good filing system.

The one thing I simply wanted no part of was the pressure of the boarding house—discipline, inspections, absentee slips, sickness and everything else. I went to the office. But before I could present my letter, I learned that the housemistress was still ill and had sent a letter asking to stay away "until finishing treatment"—that could be a day or a month. I found in that discovery a firm no to my plea for being taken away from this work. Later that same morning I walked into the office to discover that the manager today brought a friend of his to help with the typing and general office work. The man is competent and efficient, and in meeting him I discovered another answer of no to my prayers.

I see I'm to concentrate most heavily on my teaching and the girls in the boarding house. First I went to my room and cried. Then I said, "Praise the Lord" and relaxed. I'm sure that as time passes and I gain confidence and experience, I'll be glad that God has forced me again to go beyond the limits I've comfortably tried to set myself.

Love, Adwoa

March 8

Dear Kwadwo,

The housemistress has returned to the school! I was so happy I hugged her. The other teachers here tell me that Europeans or Americans are rarely allowed to be housemasters (or housemistresses) at schools. We're seen as too soft, or as just not understanding the culture enough. Another blow to my pride. At least I'm learning not to take myself *so* seriously. I can laugh at what the students have just christened me: "Inamerica." (They're always asking me questions about what things are like in the United States, and I often answer by beginning, "In America.")

Love, Adwoa

March 11

Dear Kwadwo,

I'm visiting Ante Aku this weekend. We spent last night having a discussion about an intercultural couple she knows —a Ghanaian married to a black American. She feels both partners are "living in hell" and that the marriage was a complete mistake. I'm sure she's concerned about you and me marrying. A friend came by and I asked him his image of the ideal woman—the woman he'd like to marry. He listed such qualities as honesty, unpretentiousness, warmth and the desire and ability to manage a household well. Both Ante Aku and he agreed that understanding and tolerance were two of the most basic requirements while overconcern with glamor, money and ambition could singly or in combination destroy a marriage. I listened, then read them

Proverbs 31:10-31 as my image of a good wife. That passage has grown on me since my first superficial reading when I didn't particularly relish it....

March 14

... We're in the middle of the second term's final exams. I had planned to supervise some of the exams but instead the assistant headmaster gave me the morning off so I could go to the Ministries. I went and actually received my visa—only six months after applying! It was almost anticlimactic.

Love, Adwoa

March 16

Dear Kwadwo,

I had a pleasantly busy day running errands. I stopped in at the new SU office to say hello and also see if the traveling secretary—an exbiologist—*really* keeps a pet snake there. He does—in a wicker basket right behind his desk. (Not only that, but I understand he eats roasted termites— yum, yum.)

Tomorrow night I'm dining with an American couple from Georgia. Rev. T. was chaplain at the University of Cape Coast for about three years and is now teaching at Trinity College. He has been actively involved with arranging guest preachers for the secondary schools in the area. I first met him one Sunday when he brought a young Ghanaian from the seminary over to speak at morning worship. I did a double take when I heard his Southern accent and learned he's a missionary from Atlanta. I soon discovered his robust good humor, sensitivity and thoughtfulness. The friendship of his wife is a special gift. Formerly a nurse, she writes and is a well-informed, interesting conversationalist. They spent several years in the Orient before coming to Ghana, so I'm looking forward to a Chinese dinner.

March 19

Last night on the roof I heard a combination of sounds—

the loud rock rhythm of some soul music being belted out at nearby Hotel de Naomi, the drumming and singing of a spiritual church near here, the hymns of the students in chapel. The three blended together into a song of Ghana. . . .

Love, Adwoa

March 20

Dear Kwadwo,

I've been reading some books by Tournier that the T.'s lent me. He discusses how it takes time to build a marriage and how often the excitement and joy of courtship, with its sense of discovery, of sharing deeply and understanding each other, gives way to boredom and superficial exchanges of information after marriage. Estrangement follows. Each partner mistakenly assumes he knows his spouse so well that no additional effort is required.

Tournier talks too about how in the oneness of marriage there is no place for hiding things from one another, even if it's a good thing you're hiding or if you're hiding it for good reasons. He doesn't mean two people have to recite everything that happens to them, of course. He means that the attitude has to be one of "loving transparency." I can see that in our married life together the honesty is going to be especially important. Let's pray that God will truly make us *one* flesh.

Love, Adwoa

March 21

Dear Kwadwo,

Your cousin Poku spent several hours here yesterday, and Afua and I have promised to visit him soon. Poku, who works at the Ministry of Labor and Co-operatives, was irate because since the coup the soldiers lock the gates to the en-

trance of the Ministries at 8:00 A.M. and make surprise
checks in the offices to see if any workers are sleeping. He
used to sneak in to work about 8:30 and sleep through
several hours in the afternoon. Also, he was angry that the
civil servants are no longer free to take hours off to do
shopping and have to sign in and out in the morning, afternoon and evening. He wanted to come visit me, so he told
his supervisor he received a call that his mother had just
been admitted into Tema General Hospital and that he was
to come immediately. Poku felt duly entitled to all these
liberties since there's never any work for him at the Ministry
(he files letters) and he is paid almost nothing. I've seen
many clerks like him when I've visited the Ministries and
really can't blame him for his lack of enthusiasm. . . .

Love, Adwoa

March 22

Dear Kwadwo,

. . . Because you love and care about me in real ways,
you're helping me grow stronger and more mature. Many
times your love has forced me to be more genuine, more
honest and to give more than I initially want to. If it weren't
for your love, for the expression of that love in letters written late at night when you're so tired you're falling asleep
or hurriedly before dashing off to class . . . if it weren't for
an unexpected tape recording or Peanuts' comic strip or a
Valentine's Day cablegram or an album of photographs or a
book, I would've found my months in Ghana much more
difficult. Because I'm confident of your love, I'm confident
that together we're "going to make it," as Kwamena says. . . .

I've been thinking about the several marriages I've wit-
nessed from the other side, when all the company goes
home and the masks of "oh-we're-so-happily-married"
drop down into the garbage with the scraps from the meal.
As I read through books and articles by those who spend

time listening to the intimate stories of people's married lives, I keep hearing one thing over and over: Any marriage will work if the two people involved want it to. The problem of the truly tragic marriage is when only one of them wants it to. I also keep hearing, "Talk to each other! Communicate! Don't start hiding behind routines, overinvolvement in worthwhile activities, silence, religion or anything else." When I weigh what I've actually seen with what is being said, it rings true.

As I mentioned last week, Tournier stresses that married couples must be prepared to talk about *everything*. I know that it's the things that are the hardest to talk about that are the most important. I need to talk to you when I become afraid of different cultural expectations: when I use my ingenuity to prepare an American-style meal (macaroni, beef and gravy), and Afua won't even taste it, and I laugh and pretend I'm not hurt at all (even though I really do understand why she wouldn't want to try it); when I want to talk to a doctor about contraceptives, and no one seems to understand why it's necessary, and I don't really know how to find a doctor; when the concept of a honeymoon is difficult for Afua or Harry to understand. These are small things, yet I need to tell you about them instead of ignoring them. I need to tell you the happy things too.

Love, Adwoa

March 25

Dear Kwadwo,

Yesterday Afua and I visited one of your aunts. She killed a chicken for us and we had *abɛnkwan*. I enjoyed myself. Your aunt was happy that I like Ghana, but she was quick to warn me that you have plenty of brothers. (I assume she meant her children.) That made me a bit concerned because I have visions of nieces, nephews and cousins all waiting on our doorstep when we arrive in Ghana. I find myself perfectly willing to assume responsibility for Ama and Afua, and not unhappy at all about helping Kwaku with the prospect of ultimately sending him to the States to do graduate work if he still wants to in a few years. I wonder about how many people we'll be helping along. I need to trust God more about our money. It isn't that I want to be rich. "Martha, Martha, you are anxious and troubled about many things; one thing is needful . . . Seek first the kingdom of God and his righteousness, and all these things will be added to you."

Together over the years we'll have to work out where self-sacrifice becomes a destructive compromise. For example, whenever something is different here, do I force myself to accept the fact that "You're in Ghana now . . ."? Today I decided to take some cloth I had and sew a dress using the dress my mother made me as a pattern. Afua gloomily warned me against trying it on my own: "You'd better wait until Ante Aku comes and let her cut it out." Ante Aku had already offered to cut it for me, but I explained that it would be good for me to try it on my own. (I'm not used to sewing without a pattern or pins.) Ante Aku agreed with me, so she went out and left me alone. But Gloria, Afua, another girl and Ante Aku's housegirl all came curiously to watch me.

I began as I was taught (as an American!) to get the material on the grain. Afua looked at me like I was crazy when I tried to explain what I was doing, and Gloria tried to tell me it wasn't necessary. It probably wasn't, but I felt committed to finishing what I had started. Later, as I was sewing, Afua said that I cut one piece too small. I showed her that when the seam allowance was taken into account, it was exactly the right length. Then she said flatly, "You have to take that out. You did it wrong." That was too much.

It's a bitter thing for a woman to leave her home and her society and come to a new place where she has to begin again and learn *everything* new—from washing her clothes to cooking to sweeping to urinating to appropriate social behaviors. It's a humbling experience, but it can also shake a woman's self-confidence considerably. Sometimes, like when I began to sew my dress, it's important just to be left alone to show that I can do *something* well on my own. It would have been important even if I'd completely destroyed the cloth (which I didn't, incidentally).

I said something to Afua about her hurting me. I don't think she understood. She felt hurt, too, and left me immediately. A little later I went to her and, putting my arms on hers, explained to her that if she were marrying an American and traveling to stay with my mother and sisters, and had to learn all over again how to cook and sew and clean and shop and everything else, sometimes she might feel like she wanted to do something on her own just to show herself that she could. She said it was all right, that she understood, but I don't think she did. She's probably forgotten the whole episode, but it's another daily experience that reminds me how far I have to go to really adapt.

Love, Adwoa

Chapter 8
The Third Term

March 30

Dear Kwadwo,

I've arrived at the conference in a very somber state of mind. On our way to Cape Coast this morning we drove onto the scene of an accident about five minutes after a Benz bus full of passengers had torn around a corner in the wrong lane and killed the driver of a small car.

It looked, from the way the body was crushed, like the driver had made a desperate, futile attempt to get out of his auto before the collision. When we came to the spot that beautiful, quiet morning with the birds singing and everything lush green and fresh, it was to anguished cries of men, women and children passengers from the Benz who were now covering the road with their blood. Everything was confusion. We were one of the first cars to come across the mess of broken glass and bodies, so we got out of the car and loaded some of the most badly injured into it. We stopped other cars, too, to see that the other injured passengers were taken to the hospital. Some people actually drove by without stopping to try to help, and one taxi driver callously demanded six *cedis* before he would take one woman screaming with pain. When the injured were taken care of, the other passengers stopped other lorries to continue their journey.

The five of us who stayed behind waited about an hour and a half before our car returned. After the injured were removed, while we were awaiting the police (who never came), the curiosity-seekers began arriving. Every lorry stopped—or at least slowed down for the passengers to see what had happened. Villagers out working on their farms, travelers and other people came to look. The driver of the demolished car had been killed instantly in the crash, but his body was wedged in such a way that it was impossible to see his face. He had been neatly dressed in a suit and tie, and appeared to be a businessman. People were curious to see if they knew him, but no one wanted the responsibility of removing him from the car before the police arrived.

Finally, one man, well-dressed and very agitated, demanded a cutlass and importantly began cutting through the brush to the car like a madman. We all thought he knew the man. Some teen-agers, Afro-dressed and looking for adventure, helped unwedge the man from the car and remove his broken, distorted body. They laid it mercilessly in the sun. When they had finished, they all left the scene (after a good look at the corpse).

More cars stopped to look at the body. One big, loud-mouthed man dressed in a suit also wanted to feel important. He pushed his way to the front where the body was and began to make a lot of noise, shouting things like, "May he rest in peace!" and "Tsk, tsk, it was a brain concussion, I see," and "Oh, how unfortunate, this poor man, traveling on the road like this and killed in an accident. Tragic!" He was just interested in getting an audience for himself. When he did, he told them to cut branches and cover the body. (Of course, he didn't do it himself.) As soon as the body was covered, he left. I was told that he'd arrived early on the scene but didn't bother to take any of the unfortunate Benz passengers to the hospital in his big empty car.

Little by little the excitement died down and everyone went away. The five of us were warned that if the police arrived they might arrest us all and take us with them until they found out what had happened. We decided to move away from the scene. There wasn't anything else we could do anyhow while we waited for our car to return. We warned some of the villagers still standing around to see that no one stole any of the few remaining pieces of luggage from the top of the Benz.

I looked back at the pile of leaves covering the body. I listened to the silence, and I saw everything going on as if nothing had happened. I felt sorrowful. I've never come face to face with death before. I'd never even seen a dead body in real life. It impressed me profoundly as I thought of how suddenly and unexpectedly death comes, how in the moment of crisis everything unimportant is swept away and we see clearly what is important, how we were on our way to Cape Coast to celebrate the resurrection of a man who'd also been broken and died innocently. I contrasted this purposeless, tragic, unexpected death with the death of Christ. Jesus died for a purpose. His victory over death conquered what would have been a tragedy. His death had been anticipated and prepared for. All these thoughts made me more sober and serious at the conference.

Love, Adwoa

April 17

Dear Kwadwo,

The third term has begun and it's going to be exciting.

Two days ago we had a meeting to inform us that the head-master has resigned. No one has even seen the assistant headmaster since last term! This morning the housemaster finally arrived (five days late and without bothering to at-tend the staff meeting) and was called to the office by our new senior housemaster to discuss plans for this term. As soon as he left he confided to me that he's asked for an ad-vance on his salary for the month and intends to skip out soon after he gets it. He contradicted everything he'd said to the senior housemaster.

My days are filled with thoughts of filing systems, typing, notices, registers, teaching, SU work and wishing I were like an amoeba so I could just keep dividing myself over and over until there was enough of me to do everything. . . .

Love, Adwoa

April 12

Dear Kwadwo,

I'm hurting badly now and need to talk to you. This after-noon I arrived at school and went straight to the office to check for mail. Sure enough, I had two letters from mom, one from one of my sisters and four from you.

First, I opened the one from mom, excited to finally hear from her, especially about the wedding. She had written the first letter under pressure—she and two of my sisters were preparing to travel to Virginia to see her own mother. I im-mediately saw that she was hurt. On top of that (or maybe as an outlet for her anger) she soundly bawled me out for leaving the burden of my income tax forms on her to hassle and fill out. Her first line began, "Guess I'd better scribble you a line. . . ." Later she worked up to, "You asked about getting married in Ghana. You'll think this is terrible, but is it easy to get a divorce in America if things don't work out? Not many do, you know. Anyway, it's your decision, and if you want to marry in Ghana that's what you should do." She is surprised that you are going to spend all that money for a trip to Ghana with taking on the responsibility of a wife and so on. She also wonders if I can afford a whole summer of "goofing off " if I plan to go to school in the fall. She continued, "But that is your business, too—even though it seems to me that it's sort of an irresponsible way of looking at the future." She later ended (regarding my income tax), "This is the *last time I'm getting involved in one of your messes. Period."*

Long before I came to the end I was crying like a two-year-old. For my mother, who I love, to be so cold and indifferent to the questions I'd asked her, after waiting so long for her letter, tore me up. Then I read her second letter. It was a short note with my income tax form. She did have to spend several hours running down my tax forms and checking on things for me. She had asked me three times what I wanted her to do. I thought I'd written her about it, but I must not have. That note kept the tears falling. She said, "Hope you had a good Easter" and spent most of the time describing the meal she was making for the Easter family get-together. She also included a short "Love" written by Michelle and told me she bought a book I asked her to get. I know she loves me dearly and I'm breaking her heart. It makes me ache inside, especially now when I long to be able to confide in her and talk with her.

The letter from my sister practically begged me to wait and marry in the United States. I feel confused now. Remember how Ante Aku and Afua both advised us against marrying in Ghana? Perhaps my commitment to your family in Ghana is deepening my commitment to my own family (mother, father and sisters). I just don't know what to do about the wedding. I am hurt and confused. I don't want to create any more bitter feelings in my family. Please pray deeply, my love. What do we do? "I do not pray that thou shouldst take them out of the world, but that thou shouldst keep them from the evil one." Father, give us grace.

Love, Adwoa

April 14

Dear Kwadwo,

Read James 1:2-5 and note that after telling us why we should be joyful James advises us to go straight to God if we need wisdom. That's what I've done. I'm willing to postpone our wedding if he makes it clear that is the wisest step. On the other hand I'm also prepared to marry here.

I'm going to write my mom a letter to try to encourage her about our wedding but also to help her understand that I accept her right as my mother to advise me regarding this major step in my life. As clearly as I can see, I am to be obedient to my parents. I'm only called to "hate" them when their will is in opposition to what I believe God wills. In this case my mother's major objection to our marriage is the color of your skin (though it's also unhappiness that I'll be leaving her and concern for my future). God refused to make the distinction of color. His only command here seems to be that someone who follows Jesus shouldn't become one with someone who doesn't. Therefore, though this is oversimplified, I cannot let my mother (who doesn't even make the Christian/non-Christian distinction as I do) choose my mate even at the risk of hurting her.

Regarding the details of the marriage, though this is for us mainly a Christian celebration, it is also an important cultural occasion. The one who carried me in her womb nine months, fed, clothed, cared for, educated and loved me for so many years should know that her counsel and advice are still highly valued. We are always to seek reconciliation, too, aren't we?

I long to see you. I long to marry you and walk side by side with you.

Love, Adwoa

April 30

Dear Kwadwo,

I hope my last few letters show you the answers I've come up with about the questions you asked me. First, no, I don't think my mother has accepted my decision to marry you. If she had, she wouldn't still be trying to undermine it. However, I do believe that once the vows are said and time passes, she'll grow to accept it. This is called hope. "Love bears all things, believes all things, *hopes* all things."

The deeper question you asked was, however, "How much of your mother's disapproval do you think you can live with?" In other words, if my marriage proved too much for my mother to accept, do I think I could take it? To be honest, as often happens with obvious questions, I've never asked myself this pointblank before. I'm sure that's because I believe that because she loves me, she'll learn to accept and love you. However, all I have to say is, "My mother and my brothers are those who hear the word of God and do it" (Lk. 8:21). "Do not think that I have come to bring peace on earth; I have not come to bring peace, but a sword. For I have come to set . . . a daughter against her mother. . . . He who loves father or mother more than me is not worthy of me. . . . He who does not take up his cross and follow me is not worthy of me. He who finds his life will lose it, and he who loses his life for my sake will find it" (Mt. 10:34-39).

As a Christian I can never accept the statement that you will not make a good husband because you are a black man. As I said earlier, Jesus has shown me that the question is not skin color but whether my chosen mate is also one of his followers. I love you and believe that our love is good and a gift from God. Even if my marriage to you *were* to lead to suffering and rejection by my family, it wouldn't change my decision.

When my mother asks about divorce, she forgets Jesus' teachings: "What therefore God has joined together, let no man put asunder." If I yielded to my family, it would be seeking my own life and letting my family, even unconsciously, manipulate me. It would mean that my mother is a higher authority in my life than Jesus. We brought our love together and placed ourselves into God's hands. He blessed us, strengthened our love, and brought me to Ghana to prepare me to be more the kind of woman he wants me to be and to prepare you to be the man he wants you to be.

I'm truly sorry for pain I may cause others, but that won't change my decision. I'm ready to be your wife the hour you arrive in Ghana! I'm ready to crucify, every day if necessary, any self-pity or regrets that the Accuser may bring as we kneel at the marriage altar. I expect that the world will not understand us. Our job is to love, forgive and accept, but not at the cost of denying Christ.

I don't expect loneliness to be a problem. "Truly, I say to you, there is no one who has left house or brothers or sisters or mother or father or children or lands, for my sake and for the gospel, who will not receive a hundredfold now in this time, houses and brothers and sisters and mothers and children and lands, with persecutions, and in the age to come eternal life" (Mk. 10:29-30).

I'll follow. As I've already written, it is desirable that the actual wedding be performed in Ghana. Oh, Kwadwo, if it wasn't meant to be, this love and this marriage would have faded away long ago. We've been engaged for nineteen months and my love is still burning in my heart, mind and soul.

Love, Adwoa

P.S. I had a nice warm, motherly letter from mom. I hope you've seen her by now.

April 20

Dear Kwadwo,

Afua has had another sickle cell crisis. Last night Harry, a student and I read things from the Bible about healing miracles Jesus and/or his disciples did and discussed people we personally knew who'd been healed. Then I read something about praying specifically and running the risk your prayer won't be answered the way you want. Then we read in James where it says if anyone is sick, he should call for the church elders and they should pray and lay hands on them. Finally, we all prayed with all the faith we have that God will heal her completely.

She believes God loves her, but when she lies in bed moaning it makes me so sad I just want to cry. Sometimes I do but not in front of her. I've finally settled it in my mind that God can and does heal people. Afua's case is beyond medical science. Unless God intervenes she must suffer for the rest of her life. All the doctors can do is give her codeine or indocid and let her rest.

Did you ever read Camus's *The Plague*? The doctor in the book can't have faith because there's a plague and he's the one who has to watch innocent children suffer before they slowly, but inevitably, die. He can't forget and he can't have faith if it means there's a loving God who allows such ugly, meaningless things to happen. Or there's Ivan Karamazov, in *The Brothers Karamazov,* who hears how soldiers torture children by throwing them in the air in front of their mothers and catching them on the ends of their bayonets. He won't be comforted. Ivan can't believe that God is love. It's easy to say (without understanding) that the innocent suffer because we have free will or that there is sin or that the world is under the power of Satan or something like that. But finally when I watch Afua, all I can do is ask for endurance and suffer with her, and remember that my mind is finite and God is infinite. Pray with us.

Love, Adwoa

April 22

Dear Kwadwo,

It seems like months since I last wrote you. Afua has been readmitted into Korle Bu. Dr. Konotey-Ahulu wants to see what "precipitated the crisis." All they're doing besides what I was able to do for her is to check her temperature and to give her some antibiotics while they run several tests. . . .

Love, Adwoa

April 23

Dear Kwadwo,

Rev. T. recently came to preach at our school. He chose the wedding feast at Cana as his text. He described graphically how Jesus liked people and wanted them to enjoy themselves. Without neglecting the theological implications of turning water to wine, he dealt with the purely human side, too: "After all, that's a lot of wine! It's probably gonna make a lot of people feel pretty happy—not too happy, but pretty lively. They might start singing or dancing. . . ." The students really listened to him.

The more I get to know the T.'s, the more I thank God for them. They believe that by being labeled "missionaries to Africa" they will be able to get into some racist churches when they return to America. (You know, "Tonight Rev. T. and his lovely wife, a nurse, who spent three years in China and four in black Africa, bringing the heathen to the light of Jesus Christ, will show films and talk about their work among the Fantis in Cape Coast. . . .") They're automatically accepted and the staunch church member lets down his defenses. This leaves an opening for the T.'s to communicate in a way that will force him to look up in the slave balcony or stop to look at his own segregated heart and listen to what Jesus says about love. I appreciate how they're not afraid to shake people out of their complacency. After all, as Kierkegaard says, "Remove from the Christian Religion, as Christendom has done, its ability to shock, and Christianity, by becoming a direct communication, is altogether destroyed. It then becomes a tiny superficial thing capable neither of inflicting deep wounds nor of healing them. . . ."

Love, Adwoa

April 7

Dear Kwadwo,

Remember several weeks ago I mentioned that we have a new senior housemaster? Three days ago I met him in the office and realized he had just about burned himself out—his enthusiasm, smile and determination had given way to intense fatigue. He just told me he's leaving the school for good in two more days though he hasn't told the manager yet.

. . . I'm going to die! I didn't get any rest yesterday. The housemistress was sick and I still had to go to inspection last night, too. "It's gettin' tougher ev'ry morning, gettin' outta bed on time. . . ."

I didn't go to classes today. I started getting a cold a few days ago, and I've been running around trying to ignore it. Last night I had a headache, and this morning when I woke up my head was clogged. (Actually, my nose was, but it affected my head!) I just asked myself—"Why? Why drive yourself like this and get rundown and sick?" I went to the office to tell them I wouldn't be teaching today, but I didn't sleep much because masters and students kept coming to see how I was feeling. . . .

Love, Adwoa

P.S. We now have a new housemaster and also a "Dr." somebody who has agreed to be our headmaster until the term ends.

May 13

Dear Kwadwo,

... I discovered I've already had some question put on my character. It seems one of your relatives accused me of constantly troubling Ante Aku for money, and of not having any clothes of my own but always wearing Afua's and Ama's clothes. Nɛnɛ was upset and spoke to the girls. They both told her both accusations were untrue. But Afua cried that day, and I don't know whether Nɛnɛ believed them or not. I tried and tried to think who could possibly have fabricated such a story. Nɛnɛ refused to tell the girls who had said it. ...

No wonder Paul said for us to be innocent as doves yet wise as serpents. Every move I take is carefully observed by so many relatives. The least mistake or misunderstanding and gossip abounds. (Remember James? "How great a forest is set ablaze by a small fire! And the tongue is a fire.")

Love, Adwoa

May 16

Dear Kwadwo,

I recently met a European woman and her Ghanaian husband at a dinner party. He'd been away from Ghana many years, and they just arrived here last October. (I've actually been here longer than someone else!) They have a four-and-a-half-month-old baby too. I also met a friend of the wife who is visiting from Europe. The wife was a nice-looking woman a few years older than I. She was intelligent, quietly friendly, and yet, lonely. We had no opportunity for serious discussion together, but her husband was fairly open. She seemed terribly out of place in Ghana in her nice lacy, crepe dress and prettily made-up eyes. Her husband speaks Twi, yet whenever I said anything to him in Twi she couldn't understand. They said if the coup had happened before October, they probably wouldn't have come to Ghana. When I asked if they plan to stay here, the wife's answer was a tentative, "Yes . . . for now." The "for now" was whispered.

Her husband was a good conversationalist. Instead of asking the usual, "How do you like Ghana?" he asked, "What don't you like about Ghana?" Instead of saying superficially, "I like the food," or "I like the friendliness and hospitality of the people," or "I like the scenery," we talked about waiting in line at the hospital or the apparent unconcern of nurses and salesgirls for their patients and clients. I found myself defending, or rather, trying to understand and offer positive explanations for the attraction of certain jobs to Ghanaian girls and for their performance in those jobs.

I invited the wife and her friend to come to the school one afternoon, and agreed to show them the outdoor market in town. But now, secretly, I've begun to regret my offer. What's wrong? Why am I so down on Europeans acting naturally European?

I have to admit I don't like the idea of taking them to Accra with me on the lorry or even of going to the market. Maybe it's because they'd be tourists. Maybe it's because I'm unsure of myself. And yet the wife was so lonely. I could tell she hasn't made any Ghanaian friends. I'm too hardhearted. I care about her, yet I almost wish they'd stayed in England. I'm too tired to analyze my feelings tonight except to say that these women, so much like me and yet living so differently, frightened me. They don't fit at all into the life I've been leading the last eight months. They belong at the Acapulco Beach Club or the Meridian Hotel. In California or England or Germany they'd be fine. But in Ghana . . . or is this just my imagination?

Love, Adwoa

May 30

Dear Kwadwo,

... Today the Russian ambassador to Ghana came and presented some books to our school library (good orthodox reading—Marx, Engels, Lenin) and read a nice speech exalting the miracles the Soviet Union has achieved in education since the Revolution. I've arranged to visit him Friday morning at their embassy since the headmaster wants some films for the school. He was startled to hear my long-forgotten scraps of Russian. He's well-polished (just like the Americans at the USIS). I don't see how to get beneath that.

Love, Adwoa

June 5

Dear Kwadwo,

... We had our last SU meeting today. But it was interrupted midway so it had an incomplete sense to it. I read 1 Corinthians 2:1-5 where Paul talks about how he came to the Corinthians "in much fear and trembling" and how he "did not come proclaiming ... the testimony of God in lofty words or wisdom." I talked about how God chooses very ordinary people (like me) and uses us in spite of our weakness. Then I began reviewing the two years of the school and the SU group: Last year everyone was new and enthusiastic. The SU was almost completely composed of first-year students. This year there was more of a struggle with people drifting away and the necessity of developing leadership. At this point we were interrupted and had to close the meeting to arrange the seats for final exams. Immediately it started raining. Most of the students got stuck in the rain for quite a while. I put on my now-famous army poncho and went scurrying from class to class. Everyone was in good spirits except the masters who got pretty hassled trying to bring some order out of the chaos—you know the Law of Entropy!

In the middle of that last sentence the electricity went off—that makes it rough for the students since exams begin Monday—at least for those students who want to study. I have my lantern (compliments of the school) burning now, but the rest of the compound is in darkness. . . .

Love, Adwoa

Part III
Decisions

Nkakra nkakra akoko bɛnom nsuo.

("Little by little the chicken drinks water.")

Twi proverb

Chapter 9
The Ogre

By June Kwadwo and I appeared to all observers to be three-quarters of the way down the marriage aisle. However, we had yet to grapple to a finish with the most critical question of our relationship: Would our marriage facilitate or hinder our abilities to serve God?

Less than a month before he arrived in Ghana, I received a twenty-page letter in which Kwadwo shared an "emotional, spiritual, mental, physical valley" through which he'd been traveling. The letter concerned his active struggle to reconcile his decision to marry a white American with what he saw as his calling to "work towards a Christian self-expression which does not require the Christian African to become European (Western) in order to worship."

His letter burned into my consciousness anew the continuing reality of questions of guidance: Would marriage to Kwadwo be obedience to God or disobedience? Feelings of guilt and fear overcame me with a vengeance that caught me off guard, as if I had been neglecting my apprehensions despite the apparent act of confronting them during my time in Ghana. Instantaneously I suspected my confident "obedience to God's will" the most unconvincing of lies— selfish desires dressed up in pietistic language.

Kwadwo, likewise, entered into an agonizing time of indecision and testing. Alone, we re-examined the Bible, other books and our own experiences, asking God for the wisdom to discern a correct response to the decision facing us. During an intense three-week period we pitted all our understanding of God and his nature against what seemed to me to be a taunting adversary who might demand one day (with scriptural support) that we surrender to the agenda of the world and separate, and the next (with new proof texts) that we resist or consider only our personal desires and marry.

The resolution of our dilemma was painful. However, without sharing this struggle our story would not be complete. Thus, the final section of this book is devoted to excerpts from both our journals and the letters we exchanged during the last few weeks before Kwadwo met me in Ghana.

May 23

Dear Adwoa,

I was asked to speak at a rally at Hayward on "Is Christianity an Extension of Yankee Imperialism?" To prepare I did some reading in a book I have on Christianity in Tropical Africa—a compilation of papers presented at an international African seminar at the University of Ghana in 1965. I plowed through a lot of familiar territory:

With the return from Europe of Africans educated in all branches of learning, the coming of African universities which attract all types of professors with many different, or no, moral and spiritual standards, and with all kinds of literature flood-

ing the continent, Africa is being assailed by a medley of ideologies; there are militant and political ideas which are set against anything that savors of European domination or of the European's superior attitude. The result of these is either to confuse Africans or to make a good many of the intelligentsia become indifferent to, or to repudiate, all European-introduced values, or in fact, any spiritual values at all. . . . The prefabricated liturgies which have been imported from Europe and imposed on this continent have proved inadequate. There are certain emotional depths which are not being reached in Africans by these liturgies and the whole system is making for spiritual sterility as far as they are concerned. Hymns are European verses sung to European tunes, the phraseology of the liturgies are either archaic, barely intelligible, or often irrelevant in Africa. . . .[1]

. . . Later I went with a group of friends to see the Guinea Ballet. When I listened to all the music and watched the dancing, I felt very sad that none of these things are seen in any of the mainline churches in Ghana: "There are certain emotional depths which are not being reached in Africans."

The life I see ahead of me is a life dedicated to doing something about this sad state of affairs . . . reflection, questions, reflection . . . reflection . . . and what an irony— with a white wife you're going to try and work toward a Christian self-expression which does not require the Christian African to become European in order to worship! With a white wife? How strange . . . how very strange! Does it make sense?

I knew that if there were any blacks listening to my talk, they'd probably know only of the Christianity which has been used to justify slavery or to soften up blacks so they can be manipulated by whites either in Africa or in the States, the Christianity which has barred the black man from the white church, the Christianity which has told the black man that he is cursed because of his color. How do you push your way through all the various masquerades of

Christianity to the Lord Jesus?

I browsed through *Your God Is Too White*. Reading a page here, a page there, my perplexity didn't get any less. If anything, it mounted! "Those Blacks who reject the Christian God as too white and inseparably united to racist ideology and institutions must have this image destroyed if they are to have an experience with the *true* God."[2] This I totally agree with.

For example, last Friday I sat at the Inter-Varsity book-table on campus. My classmate Charlie passed by. (He's a black brother from New York in chemical engineering. We're both active in the Black Engineers and Scientists Association, of which he's the secretary.) "Are you in *this*, Osseo? Obviously he was really confused: "Osseo—President of the Ghana Students Association—pushing this deadly poison." We talked for some time. He described himself as "a Muslim, though not a good one." He went to a Catholic church a few times until the eighth grade and even tried to get his parents to go, but it "didn't work out." To explain how I could be a Christian I tried to draw the distinction between *ideology* and the *use* of ideology. But I doubt if that clarified anything for him. "Look, ideology and the use of ideology are inseparable" was what he probably was thinking all the while he was listening to me!

Last week was Black Experience Week, and Charlie drew my attention to a lecture on campus to be given by a black professor from the State University of New York on "The Impact of Africans on the New World." It was an interesting lecture. He speculated that certain cultural similarities between some of the Indians in South America and West Africans would suggest a pre-Columbian contact of the Africans and the Indians, perhaps by the Africans crossing the Atlantic on reed boats. Then came the inevitable attack on Christianity: "The white man came to Africa and mocked the gods of the Africans. When you take away the gods of a people, you have destroyed their spirit. Africa will never be free again until every head of state prays publicly to an African god, whether he believes in the god or not." (Applause, applause, applause!) Can people ever make the distinction between ideology and the use of ideology?

Then he talked about what he termed the "black is beautiful plateau": "We need to move beyond this plateau. It was important that we got there, but now we need to move on. The white man isn't too bothered that you say you're black and beautiful; in fact, he'll manufacture special "natural" cosmetics to make you even more beautiful. That doesn't bother him at all. Oh, you may even go and take his women, that's no problem for him. He knows if you're after his women, it's not worth the trouble worrying about you anyway." (Applause, applause, applause!)

Some of the things I'd been reading in *Your God Is Too White* came flooding through my mind: "Those Blacks who reject the Christian God as too white and inseparably united to racist ideology and institutions must have *this image destroyed* if they are to have an experience with the *true* God."

I know I feel a strong calling as a black Christian to work at having this image destroyed . . . reflection . . . questions . . . reflections. . . . But, Kwadwo, what image will *you* be creating with your white wife? Wouldn't it be self-defeating?

Love, Kwadwo

May 31

Kwadwo, my love,

I read your letter again and again. I've thought of all our times together. I've thought and thought. I'm being torn apart. After I read your letter I fell on my knees and poured out my heart and tears to our Father. All day since then I've been plunging further and further downwards, but it seems I'm seeing with a strange clearness. And this is my vision.

As I pondered your reflections, the thought—hidden away since long before I came to Ghana—screamed inside my heart and brain, "You can't marry Kwadwo!" I can't get free of it. "A man is a man and a woman a woman, but black and white together is an ideological statement." That keeps ringing in my ears. My people have trod and killed and cursed and raped and now my skin is a stumbling block to my black brothers and sisters whether they reject me or not.

Kwadwo, my marriage to you would be a denial of my love for others. It would be a betrayal of you. You are one of the men who really sees what the issue is. Many Ghanaian Christians say easily, "Race doesn't make any difference. We're all Christians." They don't even recognize the problem. I'm not sure I'm being clear. How badly Ghana needs you and your vision. If you come with *me*— I don't care how good or how different I try to be—you'll fit right into the stereotype. You'd *never* get through to those who're turned off now to the white man's burden (Christianity). I can almost hear the comments whispered about or thrown in your face. And you can't prove they're not true.

Surely, there can't have been many men in your position. I feel now like the sins of the fathers are visited on their children—on me. And I don't know anyone in Ghana I can talk to about these things—no one at the school, surely. No one. But how can I close my eyes to these questions? How dare I? How dare you?

Kwadwo, who are we considering? Ourselves? Or our brothers and sisters who can't hear a word we're saying?

Love, Adwoa

Journal Entry *May 31*

> Listen, O God, to my pleading,
> > do not hide thyself when I pray.
> Hear me and answer,
> > for my cares give me no peace....
> Fear and trembling overwhelm me
> > and I shudder from head to foot.
> Oh that I had the wings of a dove
> > to fly away and be at rest!
> I should escape far away
> > and find a refuge in the wilderness.
> *(Ps. 55: 1-2, 5-7, NEB)*

What do we do? Oh God, what should I do? I am confident that I can adjust to Ghanaian life. I could be his wife gladly. But is that best for him? Is it? Should I sacrifice my personal desires to free him? I love him—his touch, his whole being. It would be painful—incredibly painful—to let him go. Should I let him find a Ghanaian woman? Would it be giving in to the world? Or to God? Or escaping? I just don't, can't know.

My energy has fallen to zero. I want to scream and run and hit and die and do nothing at all—ever. I am just hollow. My dreams are hopeless visions—growing, rising waves crashed passed—now flecks of foam scattered with the sand. Everything black and white? It can't be. World, will you never leave us in peace?

I can't shake free of that voice in my brain: "You will never marry Kwadwo. Let him be. He loves you. You love him. Yet your marriage cannot be. Let him love in Ghana. And you, you belong back where you have another trumpet calling." I feel sure. But my feelings change. Already I'm thinking of going back, of leaving Ghana, of all the embarrassment and humiliation and pain—to him, to me. I don't know what to write him, what to say. How ready are the theories. How hard to be misunderstood.

June 1

Dear Kwadwo,

After reading your letter I was driven to search out some books and read or reread them. Among others I collected *Soul on Ice* and *Black Rage*.

Cleaver starts his book talking about me—"The Ogre" (the white woman): "I tried to repudiate the Ogre, root it out of my heart as I had done God, Constitution, principles, morals, and values—but the Ogre had its claws buried in the core of my being and refused to let go. I fought frantically to be free, but the Ogre only mocked me and sank its claws deeper into my soul. . . . I, a black man, confronted the Ogre—the white woman."[3] He ends his book with a passionate love letter "To All Black Women, from All Black Men": "For four hundred years you have been a woman alone, bereft of her man, a manless woman. . . ."[4]

In *Black Rage* Grier and Cobbs have a chapter on "Achieving Womanhood," and there is the standard emphasis on hair. Of course we all know that white standards of beauty mean hair-straightening. Of course we know too that with Afro-styles the natural has superseded that. But I think of how every day the girls look lovingly on my brown hair and ask me to cut it and make a wig for them, or how they just want to touch it or tell me over and over how they like it.

I'm haunted by a thousand other memories too: like this afternoon when a German woman visiting at the Estates near here walked over to see me. While she was here it began to rain, and the friend with whom she's been staying (who didn't know where Olga had been walking) drove over to see if she was at my place. She drove her hot red Italian sports car right up to the dormitory, came out looking chic, and stood on the porch chatting with Olga and me before they both jumped into the car and drove away . . . followed by the infatuated looks of the girls. One begged me, "Tell her I'll be her friend." I felt sick.

Also, just this morning I was talking to a student—one of the best students in his class—who insists he wants to marry a white woman. ("They're more gentle, more honest," and so on.) I remember, too, the Ghanaian storekeeper who proudly showed me the photographs of his white girl friend in France, and passionately told me how he wished he could marry a white woman and get away from Ghana forever . . . or the two Ghanaian women I met after classes today who told me they'd like nothing better than to get out of Ghana to the States and freedom . . . or even an American missionary's unconsciously patronizing remark, "He probably chose to marry you because he can't find any Ghanaian women of the caliber he wants."

So many images flash through my scattered mind, things I've tried to ignore by thrusting up the inevitable, "But I'm not like them." Still, I'm white, Kwadwo. The revolution of black consciousness hasn't reached this school yet. And I can't speak about it. As a white person I can't—just can't—set myself up as the authority. In fact an underlying fear of my black sisters is still kicking me. I'm still the fair-skinned, blue-eyed, noble Christian woman coming to help the poor, struggling African. I'm still the white Christian patron of the Scripture Union. And I feel like I don't fit.

My head is aching—pounding and pounding. The weight of complexity is crushing down on me. Oh, Kwadwo, how are you? Come quickly so we can speak these agonies to each other.

Love, Adwoa

June 2

Dear Kwadwo,

Am I not a free man? *Am I not an apostle? Did I not see Jesus our Lord? . . .*

To those who put me in the dock this is my answer: Have I no right to eat and drink? Have I no right to take a Christian wife about with me, like the rest of the apostles and the Lord's brothers, and Cephas? . . . If you allow others these rights, have not we a stronger claim?

But I have availed myself of no such right. On the contrary, I put up with all that comes my way rather than offer any hindrance to the gospel of Christ. . . .

I am a free man and own no master; but I have made myself every man's servant, to win over as many as possible. . . . To win Gentiles, who are outside the law, I made myself like one of them, although I am not in truth outside God's law, being under the law of Christ. To the weak I became weak, to win the weak. Indeed, I have become everything in turn to men of every sort, so that in one way or another I may save some. All this I do for the sake of the Gospel, to bear my part in proclaiming it.

You know (do you not?) that at the sports all the runners run the race, though only one wins the prize. Like them, run to win! But every athlete goes into strict training. They do it to win a fading wreath; we, a wreath that never fades. For my part, I run with a clear goal before me; I am like a boxer who does not beat the air; I bruise my own body and make it know its master, for fear that after preaching to others I should find myself rejected. . . .

"What?" you say, "is my freedom to be called in question by another man's conscience? If I partake with thankfulness, why am I blamed . . . ?" Well . . . whatever you are doing, do all for the honour of God: give no offence to Jews, or Greeks, or to the church of God. For my part I always try to meet everyone halfway, regarding not my own good, but the good of the many, so that they may be saved. Follow my example as I follow Christ's.

(From 1 Cor. 9—11, NEB)

These are heavy words sinking like stones into a bottomless well.

I pray you're strong and healthy now. Keep the faith, my brother. And know I love you.

Adwoa

Kwadwo's Journal Entry *June 9*

I think of Abraham trudging up the hill with his son Isaac. His dearest son he was ready to give up for the Lord. I think of me, trudging up the hill of faith, with my dearest possession: my reputation and pride in hand ready to give up for the Lord.

But, like Abraham, the Lord provided his own sacrifice. He said, "Mission accomplished. Now that you've shown you're willing to sacrifice your reputation and pride for my sake, now here's the task ahead for you."

There are two things I see. For the white Christian to demonstrate the love of Jesus, he must prove that he's free of the racial hang-ups his parents had. For the black Christian to demonstrate true Christianity, he must prove that he is free of the racial hang-ups his parents or the black church had.

The two correctives seem to require the opposite action. The black Christian must demonstrate that God does not work only with whites, that is, try to do some things without white sponsorship. The white Christian must demonstrate that God does not use only whites, that is, extend his circle of involvement toward the black community.

For the white Christian, relative engagement; for the black Christian, relative disengagement.

Kwadwo's Journal Entry *June 10*

Until now, the dominant theme has been, "My strength is found in weakness." When we're most vulnerable, then is God's name lifted high:

For it seems to me God has made us apostles the most abject of mankind. We are like men condemned to death in the arena, a spectacle to the whole universe—angels as well as men. We are fools for Christ's sake, while you are such sensible Christians. We are weak; you are so powerful. We are in disgrace; you are honoured.... They slander us, and we humbly make our appeal.... *(1 Cor. 4:9-13, NEB)*

But now, for some strange reason, my mind doesn't seem to be able to shake itself free of this other theme:

"We are free to do anything," you say. Yes, but is everything good for us? "We are free to do anything," but does everything help the building of the community? Each of you must regard, not his own interests, but the other man's. . . .

"What?" you say, "is my freedom to be called in question by another man's conscience?" . . . Well, whether you eat or drink, or whatever you are doing, do all for the honour of God: give no offence to Jews, or Greeks, or to the church of God. For my part I always try to meet everyone half-way, regarding not my own good but the good of the many, so that they may be saved. Follow my example as I follow Christ's. *(1 Cor. 10:23-24, 30–11:1, NEB)*

I think of when the Evil One used Scripture to tempt the Lord: Could it be what I'm experiencing now is a similar phenomenon? Is he asking me, "Kwadwo, don't you think it would be more reasonable and consistent to embark on this task (clarifying the issue as to what is the gospel and what is Western culture) with all encumbrances removed–including a white wife?" Then, like Jesus, should I respond by quoting from Scripture? "Scripture says, 'I will destroy the wisdom of the wise, and bring to nothing the cleverness of the clever' " (1 Cor. 1:19, NEB).

Could it be that God's solution to the problem before us–the dignity of the black man and the purity of the gospel–actually includes this: to take the bull by both horns, to bring together a black man who will not bow to the white man and a white woman who, rejecting the superior attitude of her people, will be willing to incorporate significant elements of the African personality into her outlook? Could this be God's radical solution to this nebulous problem?

"This doctrine of the cross is sheer folly to those on their way to ruin, but to us who are on the way to salvation it is the power of God." (1 Cor. 1:18, NEB).

It has always been the case that God's solutions to man's problems have appeared to man as nonsolutions: Impossible, just complicating the matter further.

"Jews call for miracles, Greeks look for wisdom." Why then did Jesus have to die on the cross "a stumbling-block to Jews and folly to Greeks" (1 Cor. 1:22-23, NEB)?

Divine folly is wiser than the wisdom of man, and divine weakness stronger than man's strength. . . . To shame the wise, God has chosen what the world counts folly, and to shame what is strong, God has chosen what the world counts weakness. . . .

And yet I do speak words of wisdom, . . . not a wisdom belonging to this passing age, nor to any of its governing powers, which are declining to their end; I speak God's hidden wisdom, his secret purpose framed from the very beginning to bring us to our full glory. The powers that rule the world have never known it; if they had, they would not have crucified the Lord of glory. But, in the words of Scripture, "Things beyond our seeing, things beyond our hearing, things beyond our imagining, all prepared by God for those who love him," these it is that God has revealed to us through the Spirit. *(1 Cor. 1:25, 27; 2:6-10, NEB)*

June 4

Dear Kwadwo,

May the Lord grant us both his wisdom and his peace.

I am now seriously questioning whether or not I should become your wife. I don't question our love but rather the expression of that love. I realize now what a handicap I would be to you. Even in my love for you I can't change my background or upbringing. I'm from a highly competitive, individualistic, industrialized and often imperialistic country. Ghana is communal, agricultural, developing.

You know how over the months of September to January

during my last year at the University of California our relationship gradually deepened until I knew I loved you. I loved you enough to risk everything I was and am to be your wife. You know it was my love for you that carried me through the agonized confrontation with my mom, the hectic months working two jobs and going to school, the uncertainty of coming to Ghana and finding a job, the nine months of separation we've had, and the sometimes bewildering new experiences. I've learned more about myself here at MODESCO—teaching, being put in a totally new environment where I'm like a baby, trying to work out my discipleship in terms of working with the Scripture Union, being assistant housemistress and helping in the office—than I did in most of my time at the university. I think I'm learning to face my weaknesses more honestly and realistically too. And because of my love for you, I'm being forced into a crisis of decision.

Do we say, "With men this is impossible, but with God all things are possible" and marry? Do we pray we'll be the exception and choose to marry in spite of the racial and cultural conflicts? Or do we separate before the irrevocable step is taken? Up to now I've said, "Continue with your hand to the plowshare." But we have to consider whether we'll be able to complete the tower once we begin it. I'm not unstable or unreliable, but I've had a chance to taste the cost, and it makes me afraid. True, Jesus said we have to be prepared to leave mother and father, sisters and brothers for his sake and the sake of the gospel. But can we truly say we are marrying out of obedience? We'll both be speaking the gospel wherever we are. And would any suffering really be because of our love for Jesus or simply our love for each other? Would our witness be helped or hindered by our marriage?

I know of your love for me, Kwadwo. You've shown me again and again and again almost every day in another letter, in a thoughtful book or in a photograph. I can't share what it has all meant to me, especially in the lonely hours. Or the lovesick hours.

And yet what do I say to you now? I'm not sure we'll make it? If you want to set up a model Ghanaian family you'll never be able to. I'm a WASP, my love. I'm not Ghanaian. Though I like *fufu* very much, it's not my natural food. Yes, all those Western things like toast and coffee and cheese and salads are wrong in Ghana. My long, flowing hair is wrong in Ghana. My folksongs and history don't belong to Ghana. Mascara and blue jeans don't belong in Ghana. Sunday outings to the beach are wrong in Ghana. And if we returned to a university setting, ideology and the use of ideology would be much more important than in this fishing town.

If you married me, you would be unavoidably undertaking a task in learning to understand me and compromising with me. I'm bound to feel homesick and misunderstood sometimes. One European Christian married to a Ghanaian told me she spent many years and two extended trips back to England to get adjusted to living here, and I wouldn't say she's happy even now. How would you like having to return to the States with me if one day I decided I needed a chance to see the United States again? You see the possible difficulties? To marry a Ghanaian would make life infinitely less complicated.

Perhaps who I am is just too inextricably bound up with my American background. It's the little things that build up. When I want to share with someone I find Mrs. T. understands more than any Ghanaian I've met, including your brother or sisters, Harry or Grace. The reason must be that we share similar backgrounds. Also, surely I'm missing much of you that a Ghanaian woman could touch.

Kwadwo, I'm sorry. The tears have burned down my fiery cheeks already. I can't bear to wait three weeks to hear from you. And I'm even more afraid that the minute your fingers touch mine, all these letters and thoughts will be snuffed out in the passion of the minute. It's no use to deny it. I long to be surrounded by your love. But I know the passion will ebb some day.

Love, Adwoa

Kwadwo's Journal Entry *June 11*

My mind is like a pendulum. Swing it in all kinds of directions, sooner or later it finds its resting place at one point.

I've allowed my mind to wander, to explore, to dig, to sink deep down, to look under stones. And, like the pendulum, it seems to return after each inner exploration to the same resting point. The more deeply I dig, the more vigorous is this rebound:

You have to demonstrate that some white Christians are not like that. *I have to demonstrate that some black Christians are not like* that.

Ours shall be the love which shall not find its consummation on the marriage bed.

Now you don't find anyone in Ghana you can talk with about these things. And I on my part don't find anyone here in the States whom I think would understand these things. I trust that out of our experience together others, both in Ghana and the States, will find someone they can talk with should they find themselves in a similar situation.

Chapter 10
Resolution

Kwadwo's Journal Entry *June 13*

An Encounter with Kierkegaard: Fellow Traveler on the Way of the Cross:

It is very dangerous to go into eternity with possibilities which oneself prevented from becoming realities. A possibility is a hint from God. One must follow it. In every man there is latent the highest possibility; one must follow it.If God does not wish it then let him prevent it, but one must not hinder oneself. Trusting to God I have dared, but I was not successful; in that is to be found peace, calm, and confidence in God. I have not dared: that is a woeful thought, a torment in eternity.[1]

These two candles of love, shall they be snuffed out? No! But they will be placed on new stands where they will shine brightest. That is the way I see my relationship with Adwoa going.

The Word tells us that "in everything God works for good with those who love him." Every moment of our lives therefore has meaning and must be viewed not as a segmented episode but as part of a continuum extending from God to God. Our experiences have meaning precisely because we are people on a journey and every step we take with the Master brings us closer to our destination.

Experience, it is said, makes a man wise. That is very silly talk. If there were nothing beyond experience it would simply drive him mad.[2]

As I reflect on our love story, it is clear to me that because we see all that has transpired as part of a continuum, our experience will not drive us mad. The Lord be praised. Do I have any regrets about having taken a step which now I cannot continue? Not at all: "For what is it that I desire? I desire to be educated spiritually—and yet I do not desire to act decisively? Nonsense."[3]

Jesus himself said, "If you dwell within the revelation I have brought . . . you shall know the truth, and the truth will set you free" (Jn. 8:31-32, NEB). There are no proofs beforehand!

. . . And so I say to myself: I choose, . . . I decide to stake my whole life upon that *if.* Then he lives; lives entirely full of the idea, risking his life for it: and his life is the proof that he believes. He did not have a few proofs, and so believed and then began to live. No, the very reverse.

That is called risking; and without risk faith is an impossibility. To be related to [the] spirit means to undergo a test; to believe, to wish to believe, is to change one's life into a trial; daily test is the trial of faith.[4]

"Trusting to God, I have dared. . . . If God does not wish it then let him prevent it. . . ." And it seems he has; I see our lives as two circles: touching but never to meet. Having come so close to each other and then having to part again, our love unconsummated is not a light thing for either of us. As she wrote in the letter I received yesterday,

The tears have burned down my fiery cheeks already. I can't bear to wait three weeks to hear from you. And I'm even more afraid that the minute your fingers touch mine, all these letters and thoughts will be snuffed out in the passion of the minute. It's no use to deny it. I long to be surrounded by your love.

"It's no use to deny it. I long to be surrounded by your love"—Adwoa.

You say: she was beautiful. Oh what do you know about it; I know it, for her beauty cost me tears—I myself bought flowers with which to adorn her, I would have hung all the adornments of the world upon her, though only as they served to bring out all the hidden beauty within—and as she stood there in her array—I had to go—as her [joyful] look, so full of life, met mine—I had to go—and I went out and wept bitterly.[5]

She ended her letter, "Love, Adwoa." The passion will ebb some day . . . but will the love? No, but not the love we thought it would be. In this context these words from a poem she wrote me in April a year ago sound almost prophetic: "Our love was meant for this, to help him heal his world." How prophetic. "How sweet these too-short moments," she wrote. But precisely because our love was meant to be integrated into his work of healing, precisely because of this, we shall have to let go of each other "to face this angry broken world." This past year has been part of the preparation we need for this task:

Remembering that Christ endured bodily suffering, you must arm yourselves with a temper of mind like his. When a man has thus endured bodily suffering he has finished with sin, and for the rest of his days on earth he may live, not for the things that men desire, but for what God wills. *(1 Pet. 4:1-2, NEB)*

When a man, particularly in adversity, proves himself to have been beautifully constructed, like some fine old instrument, so that with each new adversity not only are the strings unharmed but a new string added, that is a sign that the grace of God is upon him.[6]

. . . You may for a short time have to bear being plagued by all sorts of trials; so that, when Jesus Christ is revealed, your faith will have been tested and proved like gold—only it is more precious than gold, which is corruptible even though it bears testing by fire—and then you will have praise and glory and honor. *(1 Pet. 1:6-7, JB)*

Pascal says: it is so difficult to believe because it is so difficult to suffer.[7]

Kwadwo's Journal Entry *June 14*

I Too Have the Spirit (9:00 A.M.)

When it comes to purely doctrinal questions, we say, "The Lord says. . . ." There is no way around it, because he has spoken, "The Word became flesh."

When we interpret the doctrine into our existential situation, however, as when out of our doctrinal perspective we make a socio-theological statement, then like Paul we have to say, "I have no command of the Lord, but . . . I think that I have the Spirit of God" (1 Cor. 7:25, 40). The Lord spoke then. Now, it is the Spirit who is speaking, and "the wind blows where it wills, and you hear the sound of it, but you do not know whence it comes or whither it is going; so it is with every one who is born of the Spirit" (Jn. 3:8).

We do not claim infallibility: "We see in a mirror dimly, but then face to face" (1 Cor. 13:12). That is the Christian perspective. Because we see through a mirror dimly we have to walk by faith not by sight. We are learning with each new day to interpret our existence from this perspective.

On Knowing God's Will

I can never remember numbers! I believe the current understanding is that we have only five senses. Only five senses. Believe me, it is a good thing God does not always communicate with us through all five at the same time. The few occasions when it has come too close to that, the poor humans have almost been wiped out.

Recall Paul's experience on the road to Damascus. That zealous anti-Christian saw this flashing light and heard a voice—it was too much. He became temporarily blind. His whole life suddenly underwent a tremendous upheaval. What an intense experience! He spent days with Ananias trying to straighten things out. And then three more years in Arabia putting the bits and pieces together.

It is a terrible thing to fall into the hands of the Living God. Imagine God actually touching you physically like we humans do. A woman receives her first physical contact with the man she has loved secretly for a long time—what an explosion! What a bonfire! A little child, afraid of snakes, accidentally tramples on one. What shock! And imagine God touching you! No wonder the Old Testament mentions that one cannot see God and live! The times man has come closest to it, he has died or almost died. His senses were supersaturated with life!

2:30 P.M.

At lunchtime I received another set of letters from the woman I love—the woman I wanted to marry—and want to marry? and will marry? What a trip! She too seems to be going through cycles of decision and indecision. "To believe, to wish to believe, is to change one's life into a trial, daily test is the trial of faith." How very true!

Daily test. Sometimes it seems like things would be much simpler if "knowing the will of God" meant being handed a detailed road map. And yet God in his wisdom apparently does not operate that way. Being handed a road map would be like knowing everything all at once! It would be terrifying—our senses would be supersaturated. We would die. God is wise. If he shows us everything at once, it would take us all eternity to recuperate from the sheer impact of the disclosure on our senses. Where then shall we find the time to do the very thing concerning which we so urgently wanted to find his will! God is wise. His will, in this context, is like a rolled carpet unfolding with each new day. "Each day has enough trouble of its own," Jesus said (Mt. 6:34, JB). There's enough happening in a day to keep you busy twenty-four hours. Why do you want to do tomorrow's work today? Not quantity; quality!

June 5

Dear Kwadwo,

I'm sitting by the fishpond in the courtyard of Legon Hall. The pond is filled with floating green leaves and purple scepters. Bright orange goldfish flit back and forth under the leaves. Someone is playing a piano somewhere. Everyone else is returning for dinner and probably wondering why I'm sitting here so long by myself.

I'm quiet tonight. The cataclysmic questions hang suspended over our heads. The struggle of the last week has been exhausting, and I'm emotionally drained right now. Can you make sense out of the letters I've been writing? Your last letter triggered, but didn't cause, this tremendous emotional upheaval in me. My love for you and longing and confusion have been unbearable. I have more difficult decisions to make, more obvious questions to ask myself. I hope you can help me clear these things up. I know we face the same conflicts.

And how are you? I pray for you in the morning when I wake up, during the day and before I sleep. I don't know how to pray exactly, but the Spirit intercedes with groans too deep for words.

I dreamt of you last night. You were back in Ghana, and we were riding in a tro-tro with some of the students from the school. They were chattering and obviously liked you very much. In fact I couldn't get you away from them to talk to you, but I was proud and happy too. Then our eyes met in an intimate embrace.

Love, Adwoa

Kwadwo's Journal Entry *June 15*

Love That Heals

There is only one love that heals: suffering love. Jesus suffered and died: the only way to conquer sin (death) is to meet it head on.

*To disarm death, one must die . . . and rise again. Jesus did that:
"Remembering that Christ endured bodily suffering, you must arm
yourselves with a temper of mind like his" (1 Pet. 4:1, NEB).*

*Do we want to see healing in our world today? Then we must
arm ourselves with a temper of mind like his. There is no way
around it. No short cuts. We must be willing to die and live in hell
for three days, and the God who raised Christ from the dead will
also raise us after the third day.*

The Proper Tactics against Tribulation

James iv, 7—Resist the devil, and he will flee from you.

These are therefore the tactics. Not the reverse, not to
fly the devil; that can only be the tactics in temptation.

From which it may also be learnt that tribulation is a
whole quality above temptation. Humanly speaking, it is
always a relief to know that there is the possibility of
salvation in flying from danger. But where tribulation
is concerned that is not so. That is precisely what, for a
time, gives birth to new tribulation, because it will seem
to the one who is thus spiritually tried as though he had
been too sure of himself, as though he ought to have
looked about for a way of escape. This again is tribulation. Spiritual tribulation can only be fought with the
foolhardiness of faith, which attacks directly. But in his
weak moments the believer grows afraid of the foolhardiness of faith itself, as though perhaps it were to
tempt God, which once again is tribulation.[8]

*"Afraid of the foolhardiness of faith itself." Could that be part of
the reason for the present crisis which Adwoa and I are facing in
our relationship? She wrote, "Kwadwo, I'm not unstable or unreliable, but I've had a chance to taste the cost, and it makes me
afraid."*

*How should we interpret our crisis? She wrote, "True, Jesus said
we have to be prepared to leave mother and father, sister and
brother for his sake, and the sake of the gospel. But can we truly
say we are marrying out of obedience?"*

How should we interpret our crisis? She wrote, "We'll both be

*speaking the gospel wherever we are. And would any suffering
really be because of our love for Jesus or simply our love for each
other?"*

*How do we interpret our crisis? "Afraid of the foolhardiness of
faith"?? "To such a degree have people forgotten the point in
Christianity: self-denial, while worldly well-being and soft-hearted
mediocrity are idolised."[9] Are we also in danger of forgetting the
point in Christianity? Could it be that we really haven't come to
terms with the fact that "anybody who tries to live in devotion to
Christ is certain to be attacked" (2 Tim. 3:12, JB).*

Kwadwo's Journal Entry *June 16*

One Must Take the World As It Is

... Life is what one makes of it, though of course understood to mean: one must take the world as it is, that is the
content of the life of all these millions of sample-men
and of life.

Existence does not really notice the existence of all
these millions, where existence is concerned, the same
thing happens to the sample-man as to the stickleback in
relation to the net which is set to catch bigger fish, the
net is certainly there (and existence is also a net) in order
to catch fish—but the sticklebacks have free passage. The
fact that sample-men become masses does not help, they
do not in consequence weigh any more: *one sample-man
and a million touch existence,* which produces them lavishly
out of a horn of plenty, *just as little.*[10]

*It's so easy to be a sample-man–it's so convenient: One must take
the world as it is. The sample-man wholeheartedly embraces the
world view of the current peer group or pressure group. One must
take the world as it is. Thus the sample-man avoids making his own
decisions and thereby succeeds in protecting himself from taking
responsibility for his action. One must take the world as it is: This
is the popular view, and there are sample-men at both ideological*

poles—the left and the right. This is the large road, and many have taken it, for, like the stickleback and the net, choosing this road provides the sample-man with free passage through the net of existence: an escape from responsibility.

But as soon as a man with originality comes along, and consequently does not say: one must take the world as it is (the sign for a free passage, like a stickleback), but saying: whatever the world may be, I remain true to my own originality, which I do not intend to change according to the good pleasure of the world; the moment that word is heard, there is as it were a transformation in the whole of existence, as in the fairy story—when the word is said the magic castle, which has been under a spell for a hundred years, opens again, and everything comes to life: in the same way existence becomes all eyes. The Angels grow busy, look about with curiosity to see what is going to happen, for that is what interests them. On the other side, dark and sinister demons who have sat idle for a long while gnawing their fingers—jump up, stretch their limbs: "this is something for us," they say for they have waited long for something of the kind, for the sample-men give them nothing to do, they no more than the angels.[11]

Journal Entry *June 10*

The WASP woman. Where does she fit into black power and black theology? Do I? Do I?

Black freedom and black liberation are crucial. The white oppressor has co-opted the gospel and used it to keep "them niggers in their place." White racism still pervades our Western society. The black man is raising a prophetic voice, and the black Christian has a call to trumpet forth John's message from the wilderness about our God—a God of justice:

You brood of vipers! Who warned you to flee from the wrath to come? Bear fruits that befit repentance, and do not begin to say to yourselves, "We have Abraham as our father"; for I tell you, God is able from these stones to raise up children to Abraham. Even now the axe is laid to the root of the trees; every tree therefore that does not bear good fruit is cut down and thrown into the fire. *(Lk. 3:7-9)*

But God is a God of love and forgiveness and reconciliation as well. Where there is repentance (and even where there is none), there must be love. Not wish-washy, emaciated love, but Christ's kind of love–agape. That doesn't mean I should run and start preaching to blacks that they ought to let bygones be bygones–repentance doesn't come nearly so cheap. How often we whites hide behind brotherhood-of-man sermons when we mean status-quo contentment.

I wonder if this makes sense. I don't doubt that plenty of people could be fed up with any white daring to talk about forgiveness to a suffering black race.

But a black Christian can't write off anyone as hopeless, even the Man. He might have to shake him around a bit–quite a bit. But they're in the body together. As one of Kwadwo's friends used to say, we have to "flesh out the gospel."

"You shall love the Lord your God with all your heart, and with all your soul, and with all your strength, and with all your mind; and your neighbor as yourself" (Lk. 10:27). Upon this rests the Law and the Prophets.

Kwadwo's Journal Entry *June 17*

Black Power is a corrective: drawing attention to the basic fact that man has worth and dignity–and that means the black man too. Absolutize a corrective, and it loses its creative potential and degenerates instead into a destructive force. This is the danger.

Could it be that many of us are becoming overfascinated with it–making it the absolute principle of our life and defining our existence solely in terms of this corrective? We must realize that when an ideology designed to explain a part of our existence over-extends its bounds, it loses its potency.

Journal Entry *June 14*

The culture conflict. How do I confront it? ... I could try to become a Ghanaian by rejecting the unhelpful values of my first twenty-two years of life. That would mean trying to forget all my experiences and starting fresh, openly accepting everything that comes my way as better. Though this is extreme (and impossible), it's one alternative I've seriously considered and even attempted at times this year. However, it's unacceptable. I remember reading in The Lonely African *of the pathetic case of a European who let himself be burdened into poverty by the demands of his new family after he married an African woman. He lost his dignity as well. If I always cringe inside for fear I'll be labeled responsible for cutting Kwadwo off from his family and give in to every request out of fear, I'll feel exploited.*

However, if I face up to my American values, talk to Kwadwo about his values and try to work out solutions that satisfy us both, we may evolve a third system that supersedes those of the two cultures. That means I would be free to move between those cultures— to speak Twi, pound fufu, wear Ghanaian clothes one day and the next wear European dress and speak English. If I'm to be rejected by some, I need to come to understand that rejection (in Ghana I get so frustratingly vulnerable) and to try to provide a model of behavior to overcome it.

Journal Entry *June 23*

Am I just afraid of the unknown? The cost of taking that irrevocable step? Have I been looking for a way out, a back door?

As if the easy way is correct, the suffering way wrong. But is it? Was it easy for Abraham to leave his home? For him to take Isaac to the altar? God seems to prefer to make things tough. When it gets hard, does it mean God has deserted me? That I was wrong to come to Ghana? Of course not. Either his promise of being with us is true or it isn't.

. . . I jumped into the sea and got frightened and knocked around by the waves. I didn't know how strong the current was. But now my muscles are getting stronger and I'm no longer content to sink.

And I'm not alone. God has given me brothers and sisters here to help support me too.

It is right to risk. "Now faith is the assurance of things hoped for, the conviction of things not seen."

The decision is ours—we can place no blame on God or on each other. This confusion is a testing, a temptation to run away for fear things will get out of control. For a Christian, things can never get out of God's control.

I can't help but think how difficult our marriage could be. Yet I also can't help but think of the potential for exquisite joy that it holds. How symbolic of God's redeeming love if he could mold us together without destroying either.

Kwadwo's Journal Entry *June 19*

"Even gold passes through the assayer's fire, and more precious than perishable gold is faith which has stood the test" (1 Pet. 1:7, NEB). More precious is love that has passed through fire. Amen.

This is what the apostle means when he says that the Christian's fight is not merely against flesh and blood but with principalities and powers. . . .

The existence of a Christian touches existence. It is no doubt true that he cannot be said to bring with him originality in the sense of genius, but he personally assumes the demands of Christianity with originality, in regard to being a Christian, and therefore pays no attention to the miserable saying that one must take the world as it is.

And ethically . . . originality means to stake everything, to risk everything, *first* the kingdom of God.[12]

As I review the last few days and my relationship with Adwoa, I'm struck by the reality of the fact that we are fighting against princi-palities and powers. The pull to take the world as it is can be so strong! More precious is love that has passed through the fire.

The Lord said, "If you dwell within the revelation I have brought . . . you shall know the truth, and the truth will set you free" (Jn. 8:31-32, NEB). Thank you, Master. Your truth does set us free. Free to love. When we give in and take the world as it is, we lose our origin, our originality, the true center, everything gets unhinged and we lose sight of what's at stake.

"Originality means to stake everything, to risk everything, first the kingdom of God."*

Journal Entry *June 27*

I received a tape from Kwadwo today. He laughed on it and the sound flooded me with hope. He said, "We just have to live for Christ and leave it to people to make whatever kinds of judgments they wish to make. We shall have to learn to take our discipleship very seriously and live it out very seriously."

I say, "Amen."

It sounds as if Bonhoeffer wrote these words just for us:

It is wholly right and proper for a bride and bridegroom to welcome their wedding day with a sense of triumph. All the difficulties, obstacles, impediments, doubts and suspicions have at last been—I shall not say, thrown to the winds, for that would be to make too light of them— but honestly faced and overcome. . . . By your free assent you have conquered a new land to live in.[13]

Notes

Chapter 3
[1]*James Baldwin,* Go Tell It on the Mountain *(New York: Dell, 1967), p. 80.*
[2]*Ibid., p. 189.*
[3]*Ibid., p. 204.*

Chapter 9
[1]*C. G. Baeta, ed.,* Christianity in Tropical Africa *(Suffolk: Oxford University Press, 1968), pp. 432-34.*
[2]*Columbus Salley and Ronald Behm,* Your God Is Too White *(Downers Grove, Illinois: InterVarsity Press, 1970), p. 82.*
[3]*Eldridge Cleaver,* Soul on Ice *(New York: Dell, 1968), p. 6.*
[4]*Ibid., p. 205.*

Chapter 10
[1]*Alexander Dru, ed. and trans.,* The Journals of Sören Kierkegaard *(London & Glasgow: Collins, 1958), p. 147.*
[2]*Ibid., pp. 84-85.*
[3]*Ibid., p. 183.*
[4]*Ibid., pp. 185-86.*
[5]*Ibid., p. 76.*
[6]*Ibid., p. 125.*
[7]*Ibid., p. 111.*
[8]*Ibid., p. 207-08.*
[9]*Ibid., p. 241.*
[10]*Ibid., p. 247 (Kwadwo's italics).*
[11]*Ibid., pp. 247-48.*
[12]*Ibid., p. 248.*
[13]*Dietrich Bonhoeffer,* Letters & Papers from Prison *(New York: Macmillan, 1962), p. 43.*